The Covered Wagon
and
Other Adventures

LYNN H. SCOTT

《》

The Covered Wagon
&
Other Adventures

《》

Foreword by
Charles Kuralt

UNIVERSITY OF NEBRASKA PRESS

Lincoln and London

The paper in this book
meets the
minimum requirements
of American
National Standard for
Information
Sciences – Permanence
of Paper for
Printed Library
Materials,
ANSI
Z39.48–1984

Library of Congress
Cataloging
in Publication Data

Scott, Lynn H., 1900-
The covered wagon
and other adventures.

Contents: Prologue –
A trip
to Thermopolis –
McKee's Mill – [etc.]
1. Scott, Lynn H.,
1900-   –
Childhood and youth.
2. Wyoming–
Biography.
3. Oregon–Biography.
4. West (U.S.)–
Description and
travel–1800-1950.
I. Title.
CT275.S3493A3 1988
978'.009'94 [B]
87-5857
ISBN 0-8032-4179-8
(alk. paper)

CONTENTS

《》

Foreword

《》

I have a ten-foot shelf of books by authors who have traveled across America—including a couple of books I wrote myself. Some of these volumes are by famous authors, from Dickens and Kipling to John Steinbeck. I can't wait to put Lynn Scott's wonderful record of his youthful wanderings up there on that shelf among the very best writers, for he is one of them.

The Covered Wagon and Other Adventures has powerful things to say to American readers of the late twentieth century. The first thing is that we live in a very young country. The adventures Lynn Scott remembers began only one hundred years after the return of Lewis and Clark—in 1806—from their own fabulous voyage of discovery, the one that opened the West to families like the Scotts who had spunk enough to settle it. And many of young Lynn's experiences paralleled those of Lewis and Clark—storms endured in the open, wary dealings with Indians, trading for horses, dinners of sage hen and antelope (and when things got bad enough, of porcupine), and accidents on the trail. And these are the recollections of a man who is alive and well and living in Nebraska! As we roar west along US 26 toward Casper and Thermopolis today, trying to keep the speed down to sixty miles an hour, it's easy to forget that this was an Indian trail within living memory. Lynn Scott reminds us that we are only one long generation removed from the frontier.

He also reminds us that our forebears were made of sturdy stuff. At least, *his* forebears were. One cannot help marveling at Pa, picking up and moving the family on a whim, and never showing the slightest doubt of his ability to overcome whatever crises of drought and storm and trouble might await them ahead on the trail. When rough characters show up with half a mind to steal his horses, Pa doesn't bother talking to them; he just treats them to a show of marksmanship with his Winchester to cause them to think better of the idea. He also knows exactly how to deal with such minor varmints as rattlesnakes and bedbugs. This crippled, asthmatic man comes to us in the description of his son as the sort of father all children would have liked to have had, stronger and abler than most fathers are able to be in the comfortable America we have inherited. And, throughout, there is Lynn Scott's mother, strong herself and uncomplaining, sharing the hardships and Pa's hopes, and occasionally stepping forward to take charge, as when an amorous Indian tries to make off with her frightened daughter. Both Ma and Pa suffer physical illness, but they never suffer one weak or fearful moment. It is worth reflecting that we wouldn't have much of a country if we hadn't had a lot of brave men and women like them.

It is easy now to make the trips the Scotts made with such difficulty. I, too, have wandered west from the Nebraska farm country along the rivers toward the mountains and the badlands and the lush, green valleys of the great Northwest. But it isn't the same now that the ribbons of highway smooth all the dust and ruts and river crossings out of the trip. I wish I had been up there on the springboard with Ma and Pa and Lynn looking at that country over the backs of the gray mare and the bay gelding.

Lynn Scott's book will make you wish you had been there too.

《》

Prologue

《》

Lynn Scott, my father, had not intended to write *The Covered Wagon and Other Adventures* when he began it. Instead, he was simply responding to a request from one of his granddaughters to "draw us some pictures showing what things were like when you were a boy." The request was a natural one, for the author often drew simple sketches for his grandchildren, sometimes playing the game of "finish the picture," in which the grandchild would make a cross, circle, or some other figure on a paper, then ask "Pappy," as they call him, to work it into a sketch of an animal. After he had drawn several sketches of scenes from his boyhood, he felt he should write a short explanatory text to go with each picture. As the number of sketches increased, so did the text necessary to explain them, and he began to realize the simple exercise was getting bigger than he had planned. He had always thought that someday he would write down some of the stories of his boyhood to pass on to his children, for he felt every man owes his progeny some record of his life so they know a bit more about their origins. The sketches and accompanying text began to form the basis for a more complete record, and he started organizing the stories and sketches into a history of the period in his boyhood when the family had traveled to Wyoming by covered wagon.

When the first episode, "A Trip to Thermopolis," was completed, I had the handwritten pages copied and bound into a book, which I gave to him as a Father's Day present. He was so pleased we had thought enough of his work to have it copied that he promptly began to write the second episode, "McKee's Mill," an account of the two years the family spent in the mountains of Oregon. The two handwritten manuscripts were combined to form *The Covered Wagon and Other Adventures*, which was so enthusiastically received by friends and relatives that I was moved to submit it to the University of Nebraska Press for consideration.

This book is the result.

Bill Scott, Miami, Arizona, August, 1986

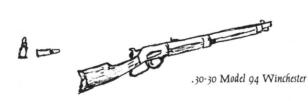

.30-30 Model 94 Winchester

«»

A Trip to Thermopolis

«»

In the spring of 1906 Pa decided we would go to Wyoming. My brother Don was suffering from rheumatism and Pa himself was having trouble with asthma. Pa sold off all the stock and what machinery we had except two wagons and two teams and a saddle pony.

After several days of preparation we were ready—Ma, Pa, and the five of us kids still at home—and on a nice spring morning we left our farm near St. Paul, Nebraska, heading west. In the lead wagon, with Bird and Tom in the harness, were Pa and Ma on the spring seat, and in the wagon bed, sitting on the sacks of oats and the rolls of bedding were Don, Bessie, and me. Bird and Tom were a gray mare and a bay gelding; the mare was on the left and the horse on the right.

There were a number of other things in the wagon, such as a grub box which fit crosswise at the front and, with the lid closed, made a footrest for those on the spring seat. The grub box, besides holding considerable staple food items, had a fairly complete set of camp cooking and eating utensils. At the right end of the grub box was the heavy leather scabbard where Pa carried his .30–30 Winchester rifle, the stock in easy reach of his hand when he sat in the driver's seat.

In the second wagon, which we called the boys' wagon, were Ralph, age about sixteen, and Glen, a couple of years younger. Hitched to their wagon was a team of geldings named Dock and Prince. They were both bays and well matched. Then, bringing up the rear on a lead rope, was our pony named Barney. Barney was brown and with saddle and bridle and lariat rope wouldn't weigh a thousand pounds. He was a smart little horse and seldom got excited; he appeared lazy but was long-winded and very fast when he wanted to run.

In the boys' wagon were a sheet-iron camp stove and a couple joints of stovepipe and a great many other things: a kerosene lantern, ax, tent and tent poles, sacks of oats, axle grease, also a 12-gauge Winchester shotgun and shells, feed bags, and hobbles for the horses.

Our destination was Thermopolis, Wyoming, some six hundred miles away over long, rough, unmarked roads and sometimes no road at all. We crossed the Loup River at St. Paul and, heading northwest, more or less laid out a route along the North Loup toward Burwell.

The first night out we made camp along the river not far from Cotesfield. There was grass for the horses and water and wood for cooking. It was a nice evening and the horses were ready to stop, being not yet used to steady pulling. Pa called us all together and said to us, "Now remember, everyone must do their share on this trip. I don't want any grumbling or shirking. Ralph, you take care of the horses. Becky (Bessie), you and Lynn rustle up some dry wood for a fire. Me and Glen will set up the tent, and Don, help your ma get supper started."

It being the first night out, we were all thrilled and happy at the prospect of camping overnight by the river. We had baked potatoes and fried side meat cooked over an open fire. Everybody was hungry and made short work of the food. After supper the boys carried more wood so there would be fuel to cook breakfast. We sat around the fire for a while, then Pa said, "Hit the hay everybody." Pa walked out around the horses to see they were all secure for the night.

The following days were mostly eat, drive, and sleep. The road so far had been fair to good, and the horses were getting used to pulling the wagons and seemed to enjoy their work. Pa seldom urged them off from a walk, but sometimes he would let them trot for a while if they wanted to.

From Burwell we followed the Loup River westward for several days. We were getting into more grassland now and Pa shot prairie chickens (grouse) several times, which we all enjoyed eating with Ma's camp biscuits.

The new had worn off travel by now and us kids were fussing among ourselves from being shut up in close quarters so much. Sometimes Pa would make us get out and walk behind the wagon for a mile or two, except Don. Don had pains in his feet and ankles and couldn't keep up, so he stayed in the wagon. After a mile or two walking, Beck and I were pretty good kids. Back in the boys' wagon, Ralph was boss and Glen was straw boss. Pa had told them at the start that was the way it was to be. Nobody questioned Pa's authority.

We followed the river to Brewster, then took off across the hills to Dunning. Along the river there was plenty of fuel and good water, but after leaving the river at Brewster, water and wood were nonexistent. At noon we ate leftovers and drank from the water barrel, which Pa always made sure was filled whenever we could get good water. Pa measured out one-half

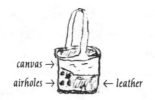

canvas →
airholes →   ← leather

*The bag was put over the horse's nose and the loop hooked
behind his ears. The horses soon learned to put their noses to the
ground to reach the grain. No feed was wasted.*

gallon of oats for each of the horses and put them in the nose
bags. He poured a cupful of water in each to moisten the oats,
then he and the boys put the bags on the horses' heads. After
the horses were through eating, we got underway again. Pa
said he wanted to get to Dunning before dark so we could
camp on the Middle Loup overnight.

About midafternoon a cloud appeared low in the west and
seemed to be growing. To an outdoorsman like Pa it meant a
good sign of a storm. Pa coaxed the horses into a trot on the
downgrades but we were still a long way from where we
wanted to spend the night. The clouds had covered the sun
now and we could see flashes of lightning down low on the
horizon. Pa looked at his big silver pocket watch. "We are still
about seven miles from the river," he said, "so we will look for
a place to camp."

The back ends of the wagons were fixed so they could be
closed, but the front was not. Pa pulled the lead wagon into a

little hollow and turned it facing away from the direction the storm was coming from. The boys followed suit with their wagon. "We've got about ten minutes," Pa called to the boys. "Unhitch your team, turn them around facing the wagon, climb up in the wagon, and hang onto the bridles." Pa and Ma did the same with our team. The boys took Barney around to the front with their team. The thunder was coming loud now and us kids lay down in the bottom of the wagon and covered up our heads.

The first big drops of rain splatted on the wagon cover, then there was a breathless pause. Pa said, "Here she comes," as a sharp crack of lightning was followed immediately by an earth-shaking boom of thunder which seemed to knock out all the stoppers. The wind hit the wagons with a force that moved them ahead until they fetched up against the horses, then there was almost constant thunder and lightning as the rain came down in torrents.

Us kids were used to thunder and lightning, but being in a house, snug and solid, was a lot different from being out on the wide prairie on a shaking, creaking wagon with only a canvas cover between us and the rampaging storm. As we lay there shaking with terror, we felt Ma's hand touch each of us on the back and Ma's voice close to our heads saying, "Pa says the worst of the storm is past."

It was still real dark for midafternoon and the rain was coming down so heavy it was driving mist and spray through the wagon cover and dampening everything inside. The next big thunderclap sounded quite a ways downrange. The wind had

Hobbles
These were buckled around the horses' ankles, to keep them from wandering away from the wagons while grazing.

Kerosene Lantern
(coal oil)

slackened off and the rain had settled down to a steady downpour. Ma got matches out of the grub box, found the kerosene lantern, and in the dim glow checked for damage, of which, considering all the sound and the fury of the storm, there was very little.

A light streak was showing in the west, and as the storm moved on eastward the sun broke through under the clouds and a bright, beautiful rainbow flashed across the sky overhead. We all climbed out of the wagons to view the most beautiful and amazing sight in the world.

The next day after the big rainstorm was bright and warm; the new grass was fresh and green and spring was in the air. Pa pushed the canvas wagon cover back so the sun shone into the wagon to dry everything out. The meadowlarks were singing their early spring song, the Loup River was lapping the grassy banks on both sides, and the bright sun made it a ribbon of silver as it wound its way down through the rugged sandhills on both sides. As we wound our way up past the newly-created Halsey National Forest, Pa explained to us that the government was experimenting with pine trees to see if they would grow in the sandhills. Pa turned to me and said, "Beansie, those little pines you see up there were planted the year you were born, in 1900." He continued in thoughtful silence for some time then, something I have done many times since; he was picturing all those rough, sparsely-grassed hills covered with beautiful green forest.

Pa
(Bill)

Ma
(Lizzie)

Ratz
(Ralph)

Glen

Don

Beck
(Bessie)

Beansie
(Lynn)

Sheet-Iron Camp Stove
Burns wood, hay, cow chips, coal,
sagebrush, pine needles.

West of Seneca we left the river and followed the railroad. "Everybody be on the lookout for wood or coal," Pa told us, "because from here on for a long ways there's no trees." Glen got on Barney and rode along the railroad track and picked up bits of coal or wood and put them in a sack tied to the saddle. When we made camp we set the camp stove up and made a fire in it to cook on. Our camp one night was by a little water hole near the railroad. There were a couple of wild ducks on it and Ralph got one with the shotgun and we had it for supper. There was plenty of grass along here and the horses didn't get oats except at noon. Days passed, and finally we came to Hemingford and Pa bought supplies of food, and oats for the horses.

We continued on north until we came to the Niobrara River, where we picked out a nice grassy spot with some brush by the river bank and made a camp. "We will stay here for a couple of days," Pa said, "and rest up." That evening Pa caught some fish out of the river for supper. The next couple of days the boys and Pa repaired and oiled harness, greased the wagons, and made some repairs to other equipment. Beck and Ma washed and patched clothes and straightened up the grub box, and in the evening we all took turns bathing in the shallow Niobrara River.

Then we went across over to Crawford. The army was still stationed there, and Pa and the boys went over to Fort Robinson to watch what Pa called a sham battle. There was a cavalry unit there, and the soldiers put on cavalry drills and different shows certain days. There were quite a lot of Indians around there, many of them mostly in their native dress. Us kids thought they were a curious sight.

From Crawford the road followed the White River up to Harrison. The White River was a trout stream and Pa tried to catch some for our noon meal, but he failed to get any. All this time we were getting used to camping out and what were hardships to start with had become just everyday life.

The first evening we made camp in the sagebrush country, we gathered dead sagebrush for our cooking fire. It was kind of smoky, but it had a pleasant smell. Ma cooked beans and sowbelly and cornbread. There was a washout a short distance from our camp. Along the washout were a lot of tall weeds with pink flowers which gave off a strong perfume of a kind that we couldn't decide whether it was good or bad. Beck and I went down there to pick some flowers. We hadn't got many when Beck grabbed me by the hand and yelled, "Rattlesnake!" We really flew back to the camp. Ralph took the bullwhip and went back down there. He was an expert with that big whip and he put in a lot of time practicing with it.

"Pa, why don't you go help that boy kill that snake?" Ma said.

"Let him alone," Pa said, "he didn't ask for any help." We

Rattles

Each time a rattlesnake sheds his skin he gains another pair of rattles. As a rule this happens once each year. The rattles to the right would, therefore, be from a ten-year-old snake.

heard a couple of sharp cracks and after a bit Ralph came back and showed us a set of rattles.

One day we came to a sheep-shearing pen in midafternoon and Pa pulled the train off to the side of the trail onto a little flat covered with short buffalo grass. We made camp there, although it was earlier than we normally made camp. After everything was set up for camp, Pa said, "Come on, Glen, let's go over and watch the boys shear sheep."

After watching a while, Pa asked the foreman if he could buy one of the sheep. The fellow, a middle-aged man with a black mustache, looked at Pa with a quizzical expression for a minute, then he said, "A lot of immigrants goin' through here eat mutton, but you are the first one to offer to buy one. Out here on the range they are not valuable enough to argue over. Which one do you want?" Pa pointed out a mostly grown lamb with full fleece and the foreman grabbed the sheep by the hind leg and dragged him over to the fence. He lifted the lamb over and said to Glen, "Now you hang onto him, boy." To Pa he said, "No charge, it's one less to shear."

Back at the camp Pa said, "Now you ladies cook up a big mess of beans and cornbread or biscuits. We're goin' to have company for supper. I invited the sheep men down for a family-style meal for a change."

Pa and the boys dressed out the mutton and hung the pelt over the wagon wheel to dry, then they propped the wagon tongue up with the neckyoke and hung the sheep carcass up to cool out. Beck and I rustled up all the sagebrush and any other fuel we could find because Ma wanted an open fire for the dutch oven besides the fire in the camp stove. Everybody was hurrying around getting ready and looking forward to having company for supper.

About sundown two men came walking across from the shearing pens. The foreman spoke to all with a simple hello, then, pointing to the other, he said, "This is my boy." They moved over to the near wagon and sat on the ground, leaning back against a wagon wheel. Pa and the foreman visited while Ma and Beck dished up the supper on tin plates. Both the sheep men watched Ma and Beck at work, hardly taking their eyes off them.

Becky handed out the food on the plates, and then Ma opened the dutch oven and gave each a golden brown biscuit, fresh and hot, to go with beans, crisp side meat, and boiled potatoes with gravy made from the fryings. The foreman thanked her and said, "I wouldn't have believed it if I hadn't seen it with my own eyes." After supper, Pa and the foreman

The shearing pen was made of boards with canvas stretched over the top of tall posts to break the hot sun from the men while they sheared the sheep.

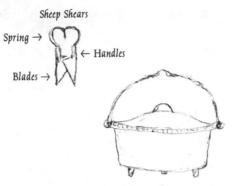

Sheep Shears

Spring →

← Handles

Blades →

Dutch Oven
*The dutch oven was made to sit directly upon the coals of an open fire. It
would cook most anything. For baking, coals were also piled on the lid,
which had a rim all around to keep ashes, etc., out of the food. It was made
of cast iron.*

lighted up their pipes and visited. The rest of us cleared up the
supper dishes and utensils, Beck stealing an occasional glance at
the shepherd boy, and he hardly taking his eyes off her. The
sheep man told Pa there had been a bad hailstorm a few days
before and a lot of sheep had died because of it. He said the
hail was a few miles on west and hadn't done much damage to
the flock around the shearing pens.

The forenoon of the following day we began seeing dead
sheep scattered over the prairie. The sagebrush hid most of
them, but some had begun to puff up in the hot sun, and the
smell didn't do anything to make the situation better. The buz-
zards were circling everywhere and doing their duty towards
disposing of the carcasses. We ate a cold lunch at noon and
pressed on to leave the unwelcome sight and smell behind.
Towards evening we found a camping spot beside a small creek
and Ma fried mutton chops for supper. The memory of all the
dead sheep didn't sharpen our anticipation any, but once we
started, our hunger made us forget all that and we ate like
travelers.

There were many needs confronting travelers of that day and one important one was a toilet. Rest stations were unheard of. Travelers had to use brush patches, washouts, or boulders for hiding places. Sometimes there were none of those and only bare ground with maybe some very short buffalo grass. In this case a shakedown was made of three poles (carried along for that purpose) and a horse blanket draped around them. We dug a hole in the V, and before leaving the next day we rolled the poles up in the blanket and filled the hole with the dirt. Not all travelers went to that much trouble.

One day after our noon meal, two Indians walked into camp. They had bows and arrows, but they laid them down a ways back and came on, the tallest one walking in the lead. They stopped a few yards from where Pa was standing by the wagon and the tall man proceeded to make signs with his hands. First he pointed to the east, then moved his arm in an arc over his head and pointed to the west. He repeated the action once more, then opened his mouth wide and pointed to show it was empty. He put his hand on his stomach, which was shrunk back from his ribs, then he stood looking at Pa to see if Pa knew what he meant.

Reading the signs, Pa spoke to the rest of us, "They've been hunting two days without anything to eat." Then to Ma, "Give 'em whatever is left over from dinner." Ma climbed into the wagon and opened the grub box. After some thought she lifted out a kettle part full of beans and a couple chunks of

This was called a cat hole for obvious reasons and brought into use the common phrase of that time, "I must fly to the cat hole."

cornbread. She handed the food down to Beck, who then handed it to the Indian. He took a few steps back from the wagon and set the kettle on the ground. The two sat down cross-legged on either side of the kettle. The tall Indian divided the cornbread and they made short work of the food, scooping the beans into their mouths with one hand and stuffing the cornbread in with the other.

When they had finished, the tall one brought the kettle back and handed it to Ma. He then stood looking intently at Beck. With her shiny black braids and darkly tanned skin she looked like she could have been his sister. He dropped to one knee beside her and, taking one of her black braids, he laid it alongside one of his own shiny black braids. He looked at Pa a moment, then leaned over and made a walking motion on the ground with his two first fingers. Beck had backed away and laced her arm through the wagon wheel. The Indian pointed to the west, toward the reservation. He then took Beck by the arm like he wanted to lead her away.

At that moment Ralph appeared from around the back of the wagon with the shotgun in the crook of his arm. He looked at Pa a moment, then at the Indian. There was tension building up and the tall Indian realized he was the cause of it.

He let loose of Beck's arm and held his arm high with the palm of his hand outward. Pa, speaking in a calm voice, said, "He thinks Becky is a runaway Indian girl and he is offering to do us a favor by taking her back to the reservation."

Ma stepped forward and said, "Let me talk to him." She then dropped to her knees and smoothed out a place on the ground. While the tall Indian watched, she drew a circle with a line dividing it through the center. In the one half she drew a hand with a finger pointing to herself, and in the other half of the circle she drew a broken arrow. The Indian studied the drawing for a while, then a smile spread over his face. He reached up and unwound a string of beads from around his neck and looped them around Beck's neck. They were quite attractive, being made partly with glass beads from the trading post, spaced at intervals with porcupine quills. With a final admiring glance at Beck he spoke to the other Indian and they walked away single file, with the tall man in the lead and the other close behind. We watched them until they were over the hill to the west. Pa looked at Beck a moment, then in a teasing voice said, "So we've got a half Indian girl in camp." Ma gave him a level look as she answered, "Better 'n havin' a dead Indian in camp."

After we reached the Wind River, we turned north and followed the freight wagon road towards Thermopolis. This country was quite rough, with a lot of rocks, and the road was badly rutted and washed out in places. The trail followed along a dry creek with a fringe of low, brush-covered hills to the east. We had seen antelope off and on along this ridge of hills. They would run from one hilltop to the next, where they'd face toward the wagons and watch until we were past even, then they would run to the next hilltop. They seemed to be fasci- nated by the white wagon covers. Pa had been studying the washed-out dry creek, and after a while he stopped the horses. He handed the lines to Ma. "I'm going to make a try for some meat." He climbed down from the wagon seat and went back and got Barney. Coming back to the lead wagon, he picked the .30–30 out from the place beside the spring seat and slid it into the saddle scabbard.

Somewhere in the past Pa had been the victim of a paralytic stroke which left one leg withered, and only by sheer determination was he able to use it at all. As it was, he had a sort of hop-and-skip gait to his walk, especially if he got in a hurry. With only one arm and one good leg, he always referred to himself as half a man. How he accomplished the things he did, I'll never know. Pa pulled himself into the saddle and said, "Now listen close. I'm goin' to ride down into the washout and about half a mile ahead. Wait here about five minutes, then come on up the trail at a slow walk."

Once into the washed-out creek bed, Pa leaned over the saddlehorn, loosed the reins, and urged Barney into a flat-out run. The little mustang, sensing the urgency, put his heart into it and cleared the boulders and clumps of stumps and driftwood lodged in the dry creek bed without a break in his rhythmic gait. Coming to a dry wash entering into the main creek bed at right angles, Pa leaned farther over Barney's neck to keep out of sight until the washout shallowed out, then he dismounted and tied Barney to a root sticking from the bank. Crouching down, he hurried to the head of the washout, which was about fifty yards from a break in the low hills.

Pa's breath was coming in gasps now and he realized he would have to calm down a bit or he wouldn't be able to shoot if he did get a chance. He had the rifle on the rim of the washout. The fringe of grass gave him a chance to see the area ahead without being seen. Antelope have eyesight equal to about a four-power telescope. They are very inquisitive animals but do not discern objects unless there is movement. Pa settled himself on his knees in the sand and prepared to wait. He could see the wagons coming slowly up the trail now and the bunch of antelope following along the hilltops. They were staying a little ahead of the progress of the wagons. Pa's breath was whistling in his throat a bit, and he uttered a few pious curses directed towards the unkind providence that made him a victim of the asthma. Figuring that the antelope would stop at the hilltop before him, Pa moved the .30–30 through the grass fringe to point in that direction. The beasts were coming down the slope and broke into a run across the swale between the hills. They can run at a sixty-mile-an-hour speed and were really splitting the breeze as they crossed the little valley in front of Pa.

Slipping his finger onto the trigger, Pa settled the stock of the rifle against his shoulder. The antelope sped up the hill and, without slowing, went over the hill and out of sight. "Damn," Pa whispered to himself, "there goes our meat." He settled back a bit and looked towards the wagons. They were much nearer now and coming slowly. Then he saw two more antelope coming down the slope. He gripped the rifle again, and as the animals reached the hilltop they stopped and looked back at the wagons. It was a doe and a half-grown fawn. The doe faced directly towards Pa as she turned her head. Pa brought the sights in line with her breast and held his breath and started to squeeze. The young one was prancing around in circles and Pa knew he didn't have much time.

He wished he had taken off his Stetson and wondered if it showed above the grass. The little carbine slammed back into his shoulder as the muzzle blast roared in his ears. The little antelope disappeared like a flash of light. The doe reared into the air, whirled, and disappeared also. Pa pulled himself up out of the washout and made his way to the top of the hill. He didn't know whether he had hit the doe or not, but from long experience he knew it paid to take a second look.

Down the slope a short ways the doe lay dead. Pa started on to where she lay. She had a large hole through her neck where the soft-nose bullet ploughed through and killed her instantly. Only the reflex action of muscles carried her this far. Pa looked her over for a moment, then he realized his breath was shrieking through his throat and he was wringing wet with sweat. He dropped the rifle to the ground and sat down on the short grass. A black velvet curtain was coming towards him. He stared at it as it seemed to slow a bit, then came on. He put up his hand to touch it as it passed over him, then he settled into deep, soft blackness.

Back at the wagons, Don called to Ma, "I heard Pa shoot. Now we will have antelope to eat." Ma slapped the lines across the horses' backs and we hurried up to a little hollow near where Pa had shot the antelope. "We just as well make camp here," she said. "It's not camp time yet, but we've got the meat to take care of, so we'll stop." Nobody even considered the possibility that Pa might have missed his shot.

Ralph pulled his wagon alongside ours and handed the lines to Glen. "Unhitch and take care of the horses. I'm goin' to go help Pa bring the antelope down." Ralph followed up the wash-out to where Barney was tied and led him up and out of the washout and over the hilltop. He saw the doe lying on the ground first, then he saw Pa also lying on the ground. He hurried to the spot, knelt down, and put his hand on Pa's chest. "Pa," he said, "Pa, are you all right?"

Pa's eyes opened slowly. He looked up into a bright blue sky with here and there little white puffs of clouds floating by. For a few seconds he couldn't remember what the situation was. The excitement and exertion had brought on a seizure of asthma where the throat muscles contract and shut off the breath. After Pa passed out, the muscles relaxed and the tortured lungs again filled with air. He sat up and looked at Ralph, then looked over at the antelope. "Yeah, I'm all right," he said. "Let's get that meat took care of." They loaded the dead antelope on Barney and went down the hill to the camp.

We were on a little spot of buffalo grass and Ma told all of us to stay near the wagons until Pa and Ralph got back because all around was sagebrush and rocks and cactus and maybe rattlesnakes. They dumped the antelope on the ground and Ralph got the bullwhip out of the wagon and whipped it through the sagebrush all around the wagons. Then he put the whip away and he and Pa started dressing out the antelope.

Glen put a quart of oats in the nose bag for each of the horses and put a cup of water in each bag to wet the oats. "Heck of a note," he told Barney, "but that's all the drink you get tonight." He went back to the wagons and hollered, "Hey! Why don't we have little Pokeyhontus over there (pointing at Beck) do a rain dance so the horses can have a drink?" Beck was always a little self-conscious about her dark complexion and shiny black hair, and more so since being mistaken for an Indian. She grabbed a tent stake and made for Glen, who took off around the wagons as fast as his short legs could carry him. On the second time around he looked back to see if Beck was gaining on him, stumbled over the wagon tongue, and lit sprawled on the ground with Beck on top of him whacking him with the tent peg. Glen was a tough little nut and probably could have defended himself in a den of wildcats. He started yelling, "Pull her off, pull her off! She's tryin' to scalp me."

We followed the freight wagon road going mostly north. It was easy to follow because it was so badly rutted and rough. Here and there were rocks in the tracks that really shook things up, and some real steep hills both up and down. It was a hard, dusty stretch and we were ready to stop whenever that time came. Finally we reached a stretch of more level country and Don asked Pa if he could go back and get Barney and ride him a while. We were all tired of the jolting wagon, but the jolts hurt Don more than they did the rest of us. Pa said, "Go ahead, but don't get far from the wagons."

We were following along a dry wash that was quite wide and deep. Don had been riding along near the rim, letting Barney nip the short grass, and had gotten some distance behind the wagons. He decided to catch up and he gave Barney a sharp cut with the end of the bridle reins. The pony, caught by surprise, gave a big jump which threw Don off balance. He dropped the reins on the pony's neck and grabbed the saddlehorn with both hands. Barney had been trained to run by sliding the reins up and down his neck, and when he felt the reins on his neck he really flew. Don's legs were not long enough to reach the stirrups, so he had stuck his feet through the loops just above them. The stirrups banging back and forth bumped the pony's ribs and he mistook them for heels kicking him to go faster. Ralph, who saw them coming, yelled to Pa. We stopped the wagons and all held our breath as we watched a crippled boy on a runaway horse. To make matters worse, there was a washout at right angles opening into the main one, and Barney was so near it we knew he could not stop in that distance. Ma buried her face in her hands, but the rest of us just sat spellbound, expecting to see boy and horse tumble into the ravine.

Barney had been called upon to do some difficult tasks before, and, believing this to be another task to be done, he rose at the edge of the washout like a bird. We expected Don to topple off in midair, but they hung together and came pounding up to the wagons to a stop. Ralph jumped from the wagon and lifted a very frightened little boy from the saddle and carried him to our wagon, where Ma, with tears streaming down her face, hugged him tight.

Late the next afternoon we caught up with a couple of heavily loaded freight wagons. There was no railroad to Thermopolis and all supplies had to be hauled from Casper or other rail points by team and wagon. Pa followed along until camping time and the freight wagons pulled off the road onto a campsite where they had stopped many times before. It was a good place, as there was water for the horses and dry brush for a campfire. Pa pulled our wagon alongside and called to one of the freighters, "Would it be all right if we camped nearby?"

"Sure," he said, "glad to have you." His voice and manner belied his looks, him being a burly fellow with dust-crusted clothes and a bristle-covered face and long, shaggy black hair sticking out from under his dirty black gunslinger Stetson. He had a big revolver in a worn holster strapped around his waist with a shell belt full of cartridges. The man on the other wagon fit the general description, except he wore a shoulder holster and carried an automatic pistol. The lead wagon had a four-horse team, and the other was driving four mules. After supper the two men came over to our camp and visited until bedtime. They had many interesting stories to tell about the many summers and winters they had been pulling the freight. The men sat around the fire and smoked their pipes long after us kids and Ma had retired to the wagons.

The long evening of pipe smoking, together with the smoky campfire, aggravated Pa's asthma. He sat up on the wagon seat and coughed and wheezed until nearly morning before it let up enough so he could get a couple hours' sleep. The next morning one of the freighters came over to our camp and told Pa he thought we could reach Thermopolis that day if we drove pretty steady. He said, "You folks just go on ahead. With our heavy loads, we won't make it until sometime tomorrow."

The road generally followed the Wind River valley and was sometimes quite near the river. At noon we picked a nice camping spot and fed and watered the horses. Pa gave each horse some extra oats, to make up for the steady travel. We ate cold biscuits and beans and Ma opened a jar of tomato preserves which she had been saving for a time like this. After dinner, while the boys were hitching the horses, Pa walked over to the river bank and stood looking thoughtfully out across the river at the rugged hills on the other side. He fished his pipe and tobacco from his vest pocket, but this time instead of building a smoke, he threw the makin's far out into the river. He made no mention of his actions. Neither did any of the rest of us, but we never saw him smoke anymore.

We came in sight of Thermopolis a little before sundown.

Winchester lever-action 12-gauge, 6-shot repeater
5 shells in the magazine, 1 in the chamber

After so many days looking forward to getting there, I must say we were a little disappointed at the appearance of the place. We stopped on a fairly level spot across the river east of town, and Pa called everybody out. By now we all knew our duties and lost no time getting camp set up, the horses cared for, and supper on the way.

After breakfast the next morning Pa and Glen took a team and wagon and went to a nearby ranch house and made arrangements to keep our horses in the ranch corral. He also asked the rancher if we could camp for a week or so where we were set up. When they came back by the tent, Pa said, "Our new neighbor said we could stay as long as we like, and he was glad to have some near neighbors. I'm goin' over to town and find out about the hot springs. What do we need in the way of eats?" Ma named off a few things such as flour, sugar, coffee, salt, beans, lard, bacon, and see if you can get some potatoes. Wild game was our main fare, and nobody ever thought about the monotony of our meals. Somewhere back a ways Pa had gotten some onions. They tasted so good we ate peelings and all.

Just north of our tent a few yards was a quite deep gully. It had no water except when it rained. Beyond that was a small mountain made up entirely of rocks of all sizes from a dove's egg up. There were no trees or anything. The ground around our camp was mostly bare and had some rocks scattered around on the gravelly soil. Up the gully a few jumps were some small trees and a large area covered with the ever-present sagebrush. Beyond that was rough, open country cut here and there by dry washes and hills and rocks on and on. There were lots of coyotes and each night we listened to their serenade. We even got so we recognized certain voices in the chorus. They hardly ever made a sound as long as the lantern was lit, but after we had gone to bed and the lights were out and all was still, they would tune up. Their song usually started with a deep-throated male voice in a soft moaning sound, then increased in volume as he ascended the scale in a series of looping yelps until he reached an unbelievably high pitch where he stopped. The sound seemed to hang in the clear, cool air. Us kids would sort of hold our breath waiting for the next sounds, which always came in a measured length of time, a series of quick, sharp yips from a female voice. Then the whole pack would cut loose.

In town Pa went into the general store and trading post, which sold about everything available except liquor. The liquor business was taken care of by an ample number of saloons. Pa asked the proprietor about the regulations of the hot springs bathhouse. "There ain't no regulations," the man said, "you just go in and bathe; it's all free, compliments of our fair city." Pa bought the groceries and, as usual, got a little treat for us kids. This time he got a dime's worth of raisins, which Ma divided among the family.

That afternoon we all went over to the bathhouse and bathed in the hot mineral water from the springs. The bathhouse was built of rough-sawed lumber. It consisted of a long shed-like building and was divided into stalls, not unlike a horse barn. The partitions were boarded up part way to the roof and there was a door on each held on by a pair of harness leather hinges. A wooden trough ran the length of the shed, passing through the stalls at the end next the wall. In each stall was a bathtub made of rough lumber which held water pretty good once it got soaked up. The trough passed over the end of the tubs, and over each tub was a hole with a beer bottle stopper. There was also a hole in the bottom of the tub and it too had a beer bottle stopper. (The reason for the beer bottle stoppers was that they would not swell and stick in the holes like a wooden plug.)

To fill the tub you simply pulled the bottle out over your tub and let it run full. A continuous stream of warm water flowed through the trough. When you got through with your bath you just pulled the bottle out of your tub and the water ran into a ditch under the floor and back into the creek. It was quite a novelty to us kids and quite an improvement over taking a bath in the cold mountain streams, which we avoided as much as possible. There was a tin cup in each stall so those that wanted to drink the mineral water had only to dip into the trough. The water didn't taste bad, sort of like stale pop, but it made us belch a lot for a while.

Pa and Don continued to take the hot spring baths each day, but the rest of us decided we didn't need to bathe so often, so we didn't go back. We washed our feet, face, and hands in the river and considered that enough. The days were warm and lazy, and all of us except Ma had time on our hands. Ralph and Glen put in a lot of time up on the rock-covered mountain throwing rocks with their shepherd slings, only they did not know that was the ancient name for them. They called them slingshots. Sometimes they would roll rocks down the steep slope and watch them jump off into the washout between the hill and the tent.

One day on the trail I had had a run-in with a nest of large black ants. These ants dug holes in the ground and carried grains of gravel to the surface and piled them up over the hole. Sometimes the pile would be as big as a washpan. I tried to fill my pockets with the gravel, but I hadn't got much until I realized the gravel was full of ants. They had gotten inside my clothes and started to sting. I let out a yell and ran screaming towards the wagons. Ma realized what the trouble was and ran to meet me. She jerked my clothes off me while I jumped up and down yelling at the top of my lungs. Ma brushed the ants off and carried me to our wagon, where she made a paste of baking soda and water and dabbed it on the lumps where the ants had stung me.

I hated those ants, so some time later when I discovered a nest being built on the north side of the tent at our Thermopolis camp I watched them for a while from a distance, then I decided I'd have to do something about it. I went over to the wagon and got the spade. I tiptoed up to the nest, shoved the spade under the pile of gravel, and with a mighty heave threw the gravel over the tent. I heard a yell from the other side and Ma came hurrying around the tent. "What in the world are you doin'?" She seemed kind of angry.

I pointed to the spot where the ants' nest had been. I said, "Them black ants was buildin' a nest there, and I got even with the summitches, see?"

I couldn't understand why Ma seemed so upset. She took me by the arm and said, "Yes, I see. Now you come and see."

about actual size

She led me around to the other side of the tent and pointed to a kettle, where a layer of gravel and a few black ants were slowly sinking into a batch of sourdough sponge she had set out in the sun to rise. I looked at the ants a bit, then I looked up at Ma and said, "Good enough for 'em."

Ma gave me a spat on the seat, and said, "Shoo, shoo, get outa here before I lose my patience." I wandered around a while then went over to the corral where the horses were eating some hay that Ralph had carried there and thrown over the fence. I stood thoughtfully watching the horses for a long while, then I went back to the tent where Ma was mixing up a new batch of sourdough sponge. "Ma," I said, "how big will I be 'fore I can make foam on my pee, like the horses and the men do?" Ma caught her underlip between her teeth. She put her hand over her face for a few seconds, then she answered, "Oh, I s'pose about the size of a horse or a man." I went back to the corral and watched the horses again. I finally decided it would be a long wait.

Several days passed, warm, lazy days. Don, Becky, and I had made us a playhouse up the washout a ways where the over-hanging bank gave us a spot of shade in the afternoons. Ralph and Glen were up on their mountain of rocks part of each day. About once each week Pa and the boys would hitch up a team and go up the river a ways where the bank sloped gently down to the water. Pa would turn the team around and back the wagon out into the river to the bottom of the wagon bed. The water flowing over the rocky river bottom was clear and cool. The boys would then dip the water up in buckets and fill the water barrel. That was the water we used for cooking and drinking.

One day Glen said to us kids, "You watch; after a while you're goin' to hear a big noise." The boys had been working around a big boulder up near the summit. They had pried the smaller rocks from around it leaving one larger rock on the bottom side to hold it until they were ready to let it go. They borrowed a long pole from the horse corral gate and carried it up to the top of their mountain. Using it as a fulcrum, they pried the rock away from the underside of the big boulder. Slowly at first, then faster and faster as it hurtled down the steep incline it began to bounce, and each time it hit the slope it loosened a ton or so of smaller rocks, which joined in its downward plunge. The boys hadn't expected quite such a display. The big rock reached the bottom of the slope, and the boys watched in horrified amazement as it bounced off a flat rock at the bottom, hurdled the washout, caught the tent dead center, and swept it away as if it had been made of cobwebs. The smaller rocks fetched up in the washout with a great racket and billowing dust.

Ralph and Glen said they didn't remember coming down off the mountain, but they were there mighty soon after the tent disappeared. Kind providence was watching over the Scotts that day. Nobody was in the tent. Pa was uptown, Ma was in the wagon putting together some things to fix for supper, and us kids were watching bug-eyed from our playhouse.

The big boulder had come to rest a couple hundred yards out on the flat in the loose sand. The tent and its contents were strewn helter-skelter along its path. We all got busy picking things up and toting them back to the campsite. Ralph and Glen were having a bad spell of jitters at the thought of what

Pa would say when he came home from town. We all helped set up the tent, and the boys got the harness awl and thread from the tool box and were busily mending the rips in the tent when Pa got home. He had seen the dust and heard the noise of the rock slide.

In a shaky voice Ma explained what had happened. Pa looked over at the boys working on the tent, then he looked steadily at Ma for some time, then his gaze traveled to each of us kids. His breath was coming in labored gasps as he half whispered, "Nobody hurt?"

Ma shook her head. "Nobody hurt," she answered.

Pa walked over to the wagon and sat down with his back to the wagon wheel. He laced his arm through the spokes. His breath was coming in great wheezing draughts, as he literally fought for his life against the contracting muscles of his throat. These spells usually lasted from one to three hours. They would taper off, and as his breath came easier he would doze off to sleep from sheer exhaustion.

After breakfast the next morning Pa got the shotgun from the wagon and handed it to Ralph.* "You boys go get some meat for dinner," he said, "and it would be a good idea to stay off the rock pile from now on." Pa came around the wagon and sat on the doubletree, near where Ma and Becky were clearing

*Ralph did not own this gun at this time. Pa gave it to him some years later. Ralph kept it as long as he lived.

up after breakfast. He talked about the rock slide a while, then asked, "Do you think the hot baths are doin' Don any good? I can't see they have helped me any, outside of bein' a lot cleaner than I've ever been before."

"Well," Ma said, "at first I thought maybe it was helping him, but now he complains about as much as ever. Poor kid seems to be in pain about all the time. Anytime you are ready to head back to Nebraska, I am." Us kids were happy to hear we might be starting back home soon, but we were to be sadly disappointed.

Glen and Ralph came back in midafternoon. "We couldn't find any sage hens," Ralph said, "but we got a porcupine. I didn't waste a shell on him. Glen killed him with a rock."

"Well," Pa said, "dress him and get him ready to cook." That night we had porcupine pot roast for supper. Most of us agreed it was better than antelope.

Next day Pa and the boys began checking over the equipment and supplies in preparation for the trip back to Nebraska. They greased the wagons, made some repairs on the harness, and tested out the covers on the wagons.

do you believe in acupunture?

About midafternoon Ma called to me from inside the tent. I went into the tent and found her lying on the bed, her forearm across her eyes. "Lynn, honey," she said, "will you bring Mommie a drink of water?"

Now, to see Ma lying down in the daytime was almost unheard of, but for her to ask to be waited upon was beyond my comprehension. I knelt down beside the bed and lifted her arm from her eyes. "Don't you feel good, Mommie?" I asked.

"Just tired, I guess."

I brought the water from the water barrel in the wagon, then took the tin cup back and hung it on the wire hook by the barrel. I went over to where Pa and the boys were working and told Pa I thought Mommie might be sick. Pa went over to the tent and stood looking down at Ma for a few moments. "How do you feel?" he asked.

"Not good," Ma answered in a faint voice.

Pa put his hand on her forehead. He looked at me a minute and then, "She's got a pretty high fever," he said.

It was a pretty glum bunch who sat at supper that evening. Ralph and Beck had got together some food, mostly leftovers,

that nobody seemed able to eat much of. We could hear a low moan from the tent once in a while. It was easy to see who the activity revolved around. Without Ma there, nobody seemed to have any motivation. Pa set his plate on the wagon tongue. "Clean up the dishes, kids."

He got up and went into the tent. Ma was rolling her head slowly back and forth on the pillow, mumbling some incoherent words. Pa put his hand on her cheek, then felt her forehead. "She's burning up," he thought. Raising the tent flap, Pa called to Becky, "Bring me a kettle of cool water and a clean dish towel." She brought the water and set it down by the bed. Pa wrung out the towel and moistened Ma's mouth, then laid the cool cloth across her face and forehead.

He stayed by the bed through the night. The fever had not subsided by early dawn, so he called Ralph and showed him what to do. "I'm going to lay down a while." Pa's breath was beginning to wheeze in his throat. He climbed into one of the wagons, propped his back against a sack of oats and, after a while, he dozed. By noon Ma had showed no improvement. Her fever was still way high. She had apparently slept a little while, because she had stopped talking and moaning for a short time. Pa removed her shoes and stockings and put a cool cloth over her feet. "Stay by the bed," he told Ralph, "and keep changing the damp cloths. I'm going over to town and see if I can get some help." He saddled Barney and rode into town.

"Is there a doctor in this town?" Pa asked the man at the store.

"Well, not a regular people doctor," the man answered, "but we've got a horse doctor. Why? Somebody sick? Doc Adams is a vet. He's the only person around that knows anything about medicine. Sometimes what works for horses also works for human bein's."

It was midafternoon before Pa got back with Doc Adams. Dark red blotches were showing through the tan on Ma's face and feet. Doc Adams came into the tent and stood looking down at Ma. After a while he looked up at Pa. "You've got a mighty sick woman there," he said. "It looks like Rocky Mountain spotted fever. How long has she had this high fever?"

"Two days and a night," Pa answered. "Is there anything you can do for her?"

"Nothing more than you are doing. Be sure and get her to swallow a little water as often as you can. It will just be a fight between the fever and the tick virus. If she can hold out another twelve hours, she's got a chance. Tick bite victims don't usually last that long."

Suppertime went by with nobody giving a thought to food. We all sat around dreading to see the darkness come. A star peeked through the dusk in the southwest sky. Bessie came over to where I was sitting on the wagon tongue. Tears were streaming down her cheeks. "We've got to do something for Ma," she whispered. Taking me by the hand, she led me out on the flat to the big boulder that had knocked the tent down. She knelt down by the huge rock and pulled me down beside her. She clasped her hands together before her face and, in a quivering voice, said, "Dear God, please do something for

Mommie. We can't get along without her. She never done anything mean to anybody, never." Her throat filled with tears and
she could say no more. She dropped her head in her hands for
a bit, then whispered to me. "Pray," she said.

I didn't know how to pray, but I was sure going to give it a
try. I looked up at the star in the southwest. It seemed real
bright now. I actually saw it wink at me. Gathering courage
from that, I began. "Well, God, you probably don't remember
me. I'm just a little feller, and maybe I've not always been a
good boy, but if you will help our Mommie get well, I promise
to be a good boy for the rest of my life."

Bessie whispered, "Amen."

We remained there on our knees gazing at that bright star.
It seemed so large and close to us we were spellbound. After
a while, we went back to the wagon feeling so emotionally
spent we climbed into the wagon and lay down with our
clothes on and went immediately to sleep.

The next morning, Beck and I climbed out of the wagon
and went over to the tent. Pa was standing in front of the
other wagon talking to Ralph. "Take Barney and go over to
town and get some beef meat." He gave Ralph some money.
Then, after a moment's thought, "Get some brandy." To us kids
he said, "Just peek in the tent, and if your Ma is asleep don't
wake her up, but if she's awake you can go in."

Beck lifted the tent flap and looked in. Ma had her head
propped up on the pillow, with her eyes open. "Come in," she
said. Her voice was weak, but she raised her hands to grasp
ours. We knelt by the bed and looked down at her face, which
was blotched all over with dark spots with whitish edges. Her
eyes were sunken in their sockets and her hair a tangled mass.
"I've been asleep," she said to Bessie, "and I feel so weak I guess
you will have to help me get fixed up."

Beck turned to me. "Go help Pa and the others get some
breakfast. I'm goin' to help Mommie a while."

I went back where the others were, and Pa faced Glen and Don and me. "Now kids," he said, "your Ma is over her fever. Its up to us to help her get well again."

Glen, who usually wasn't the first to volunteer, spoke up. "Whatever needs to be done, we'll do it. Ain't that right, kids?" Don and I agreed.

As the days went by and Ma made steady improvement, cheerfulness returned to the family. Pa had cooked up a large pot of beef broth laced with brandy, which seemed to be just what Ma needed. She gained strength steadily, but the ravages of fever still showed. Her hair was coming out in handfuls each time she combed it, and the fever-burned skin was peeling off. Came the day when she announced, "I'm ready to hit the trail whenever the rest of you are."

Both teams hitched, everything loaded, Pa took a careful look around to see nothing was forgotten. Us kids went around saying good-by to all the things we had become so familiar with, such as the Bighorn River and the playhouse in the washout. Glen went over to the rocky little mountain and picked up a pocketful of egg-sized rocks to take along to throw in his slingshot. Beck and I stopped by the big boulder and said, "Thanks, big rock, for your help with our prayers." We were on our way home.

After several days' travel in a southerly direction, we came to the main trail going east toward Casper. The next morning Pa announced, "I want to go over to the southwest a ways and look over the country, and maybe pick up a team of horses at one of the ranches over toward the Jackson Hole country. I'll take Glen with me. Ralph, you move up to my seat with Ma. The road east from here won't be too bad. Keep going at a steady rate. Glen and I will catch up with you in three or four days."

We parted there, us going east and they west. Before the day was over we began seeing Indians walking along the trail. When we got to our first camping spot, there were a couple of tipis set up there. "Do you think we ought to camp here?" Ma asked Ralph. The responsibilities of wagon boss were new to Ralph, and he was trying hard to reach a decision.

Beck spoke up. "No, let's don't stop here. I don't want to stay in an Indian camp."

"I'll have to water the horses. They have had a long day without a drink." He pulled the wagon down by the creek and unhitched the team and led them down to the water. Beck led Barney down and gave him a drink.

The Indians thought we were going to camp, and one of the women came down to the wagon. She held out her hands and said, "Food, food."

Ma wasn't very strong yet. She climbed carefully down from the wagon and went over and took the Indian woman's hands in hers. To Ralph she said, "Hitch the horses and get ready to travel. I'm going to give this poor woman some food, but we must be on our way before she gets back and shows the rest of them, or they will all be asking for food."

We made camp a few miles on down the trail. Ralph, as always, took the bullwhip and swished it all through the grass and sagebrush to shoo away the rattlers. He unhitched the horses, put oats in the nose bags, and slipped the head straps over their ears. It was good and dark by the time we finished our supper. Us kids were soon asleep in our bunks. Ralph spread his bedroll out under the wagon. He brought the horses in and tied them to the wagon. He got the 12-gauge from its place beside the seat (Pa had taken the .30–30 with him). He stuffed the magazine full of shells, pushed the gun down by his bed, and stretched out for the night.

Sometime past midnight a coyote off to the right of the

wagon cut loose with a thousand years of pent-up loneliness. Ralph sat bolt upright. The call of a coyote didn't bother him at all, but when an answering call came from the opposite side of the wagon, he picked up the 12-gauge. He recalled the tales about how the Indians used bird calls and animal calls to send messages back and forth when they were planning a raid. He pulled the hammer of the gun to full cock. He turned his head back and forth in an effort to see all sides at once. A shadowy form creeping through the sagebrush brought his heart into his throat. He raised the gun to his shoulder and followed the shadowy figure with the sights. The shadow moved off into the sagebrush, then, after a while, from farther on down the trail he heard a yelping call of a coyote again. "It was just coyotes after all," he said to himself. He let the hammer down to safety, but he didn't sleep any more that night.

The next day we caught up with some more Indians on the trail. They were traveling very slowly. Some were on foot, a few were on horseback, and one family had a team of bony horses hitched to a rickety wagon. They had stopped off the road to let the horses rest. We went on by, and Ma waved to one of the women by the wagon. She smiled and waved back. "See," Ma said, "they are our friends." Ralph didn't give an opinion, but he kept the 12-gauge loaded. We saw Indians off and on until we got clear to Casper. Each time we would pass a band of Indians, Beck would hide down in the bottom of the wagon.

When we got into Casper we found the town full of Indians and some camped around the outside. Ralph guided the team down the main street until we came to one of the general stores. He drove up to the boardwalk and stopped. Ralph had always had trouble talking to strangers. He had a sort of stoppage in his speech, sort of a stammer. He was very self-conscious about it. Ma told him to go into the store for some supplies because she was quite tired and didn't want to climb down out of the wagon. I think Ralph would have preferred to face a firing squad, but as wagon master he felt it was his duty. Ma told him a number of things to get and he walked into the store, his knees feeling like they were made of rubber bands.

The store was full of Indians, both men and women. They were looking at all the different trade goods, and now and then one would make a purchase. The clerks paid little attention to the Indians because it was impossible to hurry them. When one decided what he wanted, he would carry it to one of the clerks and make a deal.

A young lady came over to Ralph and said, "Good afternoon. Could I help you with something?" Ralph's eyes grew big and round. It had been a long time since he had seen a young woman dressed so fine, with tinted cheeks and golden curls hanging down behind her ears. She tilted her pretty head to one side and smiled up at him, showing two rows of even white teeth. Ralph's jaw dropped and his tongue slid back into his throat. "Gluck, gluck," he said. His knees almost let him down. By a mighty effort he kept his balance as the store spun round and round his head.

The girl put her hand on his arm and spoke in a sympathetic voice, "That's all right," she said kindly, "let's start all over."

Ralph knew by now he wasn't going to be able to give the order. He pointed to the door and said, "Out t-t-th-th-there."

The young lady held onto his arm and walked him out to the wagon. She knew at a glance we were long-distance travelers. She smiled up at Ma and said, "The young gentleman said you might want to order some supplies." Ma told her a list of things, which she wrote down on a pad. She turned to Ralph and said, "I'll have this put up right away. Won't you come along and help carry it out?"

Ralph knew he wasn't a talker, but he never doubted his ability to work. After a while they came back with the supplies and put them in the wagon. Ma paid the girl, then asked about all the Indians. "Oh," the girl answered, "they got their government money. They always come to town at that time to trade, and usually stay until it's all gone."

It was against the law to sell whiskey to an Indian, so the men had to make do with soda pop (mostly). The pop bottles of that day were a curious combination of ingenuity and microbes. The stopper was a rubber plug on the end of a wire loop pushed down into the neck of the bottle. When the bottle was full and the plug up in the neck, the wire loop stuck out of the bottle about one inch. By pushing the loop down, the plug was moved into the wider part of the neck, and was held there by the spring wire loop. This allowed the contents to flow (or gush) out. After the bottle was empty, the pop was rinsed out and the bottle refilled. A hook was inserted in the loop and the plug pulled back up into the neck, and it was ready to go again. The gas of the soda water created pressure to hold the rubber plug up into the tapered neck of the bottle.

Here's how it worked in real practice. An Indian man would go into the store and get a bottle of pop (they all knew how to order "pop"). He would come out and sit on the boardwalk with his feet on the ground. Several more men, and sometimes children, would make a semicircle in front of him. The pop was not kept very cold and would have quite a lot of pressure built up. He would hold the bottle out in front of his face with one hand and with the other he would hit the wire loop a good hard blow. The result was a loud "pop." He then would stick the neck of the bottle in his mouth and try to drink it as fast as it squirted out of the bottle. It was quite funny, but the Indians never laughed. They would stand around and talk in all seriousness, with gestures and shaking heads. Then, maybe after an hour or so, another would get himself a bottle and the performance would be repeated.

Modified sketch to show detail of stopper.
This stopper, by the way, gave pop its name.

We drove on through town and camped in the wagon yard on the outskirts. There were several other outfits there. Also there were some freight wagons loaded and ready to pull out in the morning. We tended the horses and ate our supper before dark, and shortly after we were all in our bunks, except Ralph, who sat out on the wagon tongue, looking off into space, tormented by visions of golden curls and pearly teeth.

"We're not gettin' a very early start this morning," Ma said the next day, "but I guess we ain't in any hurry. Pa and Glen ought to be catchin' up with us before too long."

The forenoon passed slowly, and Beck and I got out and walked behind the wagon. "I'm glad we are through with the Indians," Beck said. "I'm sure tired stayin' in the wagon all the time." I didn't kid her about the Indians, because she was bigger than I was and she could paddle me.

We found some trees and brush for our noon camp, but still no water for the horses, so as usual Ralph gave each a cup of water on their oats, and we prepared our noon meal and sat on the wagon tongue or on the grass to eat. We had all been more or less watching the back trail, but Don was the first to see them. "Here comes Pa and Glen," he called out. We all jumped up to watch them come into camp. They were leading a pair of dark chestnut mares behind the wagon and we all walked round and round looking at them. Right away we started picking out names for them. Pa said he learned we had just left the wagon yard that morning, so he had let his team trot part of the time to catch up. After noon we moved on east. It was good to have Pa back on the spring seat up front. It gave us a secure feeling. We led the new horses behind our wagon, and Barney brought up the rear behind the boys' wagon.

Some days later, Pa said we should be nearing the Nebraska line. "If I remember right, there's a spring with good water not far from here. When we locate it, we will camp for the night whether its campin' time or not."

Glen, who had been riding Barney on ahead of the wagons, came back to meet us. "The spring is about a mile ahead," he told Pa. The horses must have smelled the water, for they broke into a trot. The spot where we camped was about one-eighth of a mile from the spring, it being down in a brushy little ravine. A tiny creek flowed on down the ravine and there was brush and some trees following along down the pretty little valley. We set up the tent and put the camp stove out on the ground. Everybody was in fine spirits, there was grass for the horses and wood for cooking, it was a nice evening, and even Don's pains seemed to have left him for the time being.

Ralph came from his wagon carrying the shotgun. "I'll go get some water," he said. He picked up the water pail and went off towards the creek. It was too early to start supper yet, so we were just enjoying ourselves. Pa let us pet the new horses, who had become quite tame and friendly. Barney was jealous, but being they were both mares, he didn't get after them much. Sometimes he would nip at them if he felt they were getting more than their share of attention. From down towards the creek came the sound of shooting, five evenly spaced shots. "Well," Pa said, "Ralph's either gettin' some meat or else he's wasting a hell of a lot of ammunition."

After a bit Ralph came carrying the shotgun in one hand and the water bucket in the other. The bucket didn't have water in it, however. It was piled full of young sage hens (sage grouse). "I got one with each of the first four shots," he said, "and two with the last shot." He dumped the birds out on the ground, put the gun in the wagon, then picked up the bucket and went back after water.

The next day we crossed the line into Nebraska. We were all glad. We were a long way from home yet, but just being on Nebraska soil made us feel different. The trail reached the White River a ways above the tiny town of Glen. The whole town was owned and operated by the Cremens family. There was a post office in the back of the store. I don't remember the senior Cremens's name, but two of the children were Glen and Annie. A short distance to the west and north was the Denslo ranch. The White River at this point was just a jump across. It was clear and cool, being fed by many springs and tiny creeks from the west. The trail followed the White River to Crawford, but we didn't go there immediately. Instead we camped near the store at Glen for several days. It was a beautiful little spot with lots of shade trees, rocks, the pretty little river, and pine trees up the slope on the north side.

Pa took one team and wagon and went to look for a place to stop. He was gone for a couple of days. Ralph and Glen tried to catch some fish, but didn't have any luck. The rest of us just had fun. Ma had the Cremens family to visit with, and the time passed quickly. Walt (my oldest brother) was working on the Denslo ranch at the time. He rode his horse to the store a couple of times while we were there to see the family. None of us were in a hurry to leave that place.

When Pa came back he said he had found a place we could move into. It turned out he had bought a small ranch over between Crawford and Whitney in the edge of the badlands. There were some families from Howard County over in that area, which probably influenced Pa to buy there.

"Oh, it's a log house!" Ma exclaimed as we came in sight of the place where we expected to make our home.

"Its got a lean-to kitchen, and there's a privy," Beck said. "Now we won't have to hide out in the brush."

The house sat on a flat spot near a tiny creek. There were some fair-sized pine trees near the house, and lots of brush and trees along the creek. Not far from the house there was a small spring which had been walled up with rocks.

"There hasn't been anybody live here for a while," Pa said, "so it's gonna take some work to fix it up so we can live in it. The first thing we've got to do is fix up the corral so we will have a place to keep the horses. Your vacation is over. There's plenty to do, so lets get at it."

We unloaded the wagons and carried the camp stove and bedding inside. The floor was made of rough boards and the log walls were plastered on the inside. The lean-to kitchen had a window in the south and a door in the west. The log part had a door in the east and a window in the west, so we never did decide whether the house faced east or west. We were all excited about living in a log house. We'd had enough of the tent and wagons for a while.

The next day Pa, Ralph, and Glen took both wagons and went back to Crawford for supplies, which included a lot of boards and nails, tools, barbed wire, a second-hand heating stove, ammunition, enough food staples to last a month, and

any number of other things. Funny, I don't remember any new clothes.

For the next several days we had company: the Adolf Egley family, the Allan McMasters family, the George Grammers, and some others. These people had been neighbors of ours in Howard County. They had moved out to Dawes County, lured by cheap land and lots of wild fruit and game. The men got busy fixing up the pasture fences and the outside of the house and the yard. They hauled dry wood from down the creek. The women cooked big meals for the men and helped Ma get the inside of the house in order. Everybody was having a lot of fun doing the work, visiting, and playing jokes on each other. After they had got everything in shape for us to live, the neighbors said good-by and made us promise to come see them soon. Things quieted down and we had a chance to look around and get aquainted with our surroundings.

Off to the south of the house was a field of about twelve acres which had lain idle. The pasture land had also stood idle, so there was a good growth of grass. There were several little canyons which were immature badlands. Down in the bottoms of these were lots of wild plum trees and also chokecherry and buffaloberry bushes. Over to the west was a larger creek called Indian Creek. Every fall, several Indian families would come and camp there and pick and dry the fruit. These were friendly people, and the neighbors took their surplus dogs over there and traded them to the Indians for beaded moccasins and belts and other things that the Indian women made during the summer to trade to the white people. The dogs were their livestock.

On the other side of Indian Creek was Indian Hill, a high, round burial mound. There were lots of arrowheads, beads, and other small Indian trinkets to be found, if anybody wanted to dig around a bit. Some distance to the north was Sugarloaf Butte. It looked like a big loaf of bread. Over to the east was Dead Horse Creek. There were quite a few families lived over that way. Later on, some of the boys from over there came to our place and talked Ralph into joining their baseball team. They even had uniforms. They were bright red, with the name "Dead Horse Creek" embroidered across the back in white letters.

"Come on Ralph, let's go over to Adolf's and see if we can borrow his plow," Pa said one morning. When they came back, they stopped down by the field and hitched Bird and Tom onto the walking plow. Pa tied the lines together and put them over his back. Ralph guided the plow and they made a few rounds across the field. The soil was black and rich-looking. The horses had been on the plow before, so they quickly settled down to work. Pa looped the lines around Ralph's back. "Go ahead," he said. "Let the horses rest often for a while. They haven't pulled a plow for some time."

Pa walked on back to the house. "Well, I'm goin' to start rustlin' up some horses, so I'll be gone most of the time from now on. I'll take Glen with me. We may be gone for several days at a time, so I'll carry a bedroll and some grub along." Ma got the food together and put it in the grub box. Pa and Glen hitched the other team to the wagon, put the saddle on Barney, and tied him behind the wagon. Pa stuck the .30-30 into the scabbard at the end of the seat. He and Glen climbed in, waved to the rest of us, and left. The team of mares we had brought from Wyoming were turned into the pasture. There was water in the creek and plenty of grass.

The land to the north of the house sloped up into low hills. The creek curved around the foot of the ridge. There was a boggy strip of low ground along there with spring water seeping out of the ground. In real cold weather the water froze above and below, but the little springs never did.

The days turned into weeks. Pa brought home several horses that he had bought. He and Glen were usually home over the weekends. After Ralph finished the plowing, Pa made a sower's bag out of a grain sack with a shoulder strap. He walked back and forth across the field and sowed wheat by hand, and Ralph followed with the harrow.

Each time Pa turned new horses in with the herd, Barney lost no time letting them know who was boss. He always led the bunch when they came up to drink. If there was trouble between two of the horses, he straightened that out by driving off the aggressor.

One time when Pa and Glen were over near Fort Robinson to watch a sham battle put on by the cavalry, Pa picked up a blank cartridge one of the men had dropped and brought it home with him. Next day we were looking at it, and he explained the soldiers used blanks so nobody would be hurt in practice. "They just make a loud noise and smoke," he said; "there's no bullet in it. I'll set it on the cook stove so you can hear what a bang it makes." He set the blank on the hot stove. "Everybody get into the other room. I'm not sure what it will do." He shooed us into the living room and came in behind us. It made a loud bang, all right, but it didn't do just what he expected it to. Instead of exploding out the end of the shell as it would in a rifle chamber, it blew up like a bomb, sticking bits of metal in the walls and ceiling. It also broke out most of the window panes. You might say we all got a bang out of that.

The nights were getting pretty cold now. The wheat was up to a good start. Some of the kids were going to school part of the time. I may not have gone any; I don't remember the schoolhouse. One day George Grammer came to our house to ask us to come over for supper. "Ralph," he said, "bring your shotgun and some bird shot. The snowbirds have started to come into the millet field to feed." The boys hitched up the team and we all piled into the wagon. It was several miles over there, so it was midafternoon when we arrived. George explained, "Every fall after we cut and shock the millet, the snowbirds, by the thousands, come and light on the shocks to feed on the millet." To Ralph he said, "Get your gun and let's go."

George and Ralph hid in the weeds and brush along the edge of the field as the snowbirds came in to feed. For almost an hour they waited. The millet shocks were covered with birds and flocks of them were still coming. George whispered to Ralph, "When I say 'now,' stand up and start shooting. Aim a little above the tops of the shocks." When they stood up, the birds rose from the field in clouds. George and Ralph each fired their repeating shotguns several times. They picked up their birds and put them in a gunnysack George had taken along for the purpose. Back at the house they counted them. There were nearly two hundred. Ma and Della (my oldest sister, who was married to George Grammer) dressed them out, saving only the plump little breasts and discarding the rest of the carcass. They put a layer of the breasts in a large pan, sliced onions over them, put in some sage, salt and pepper, and water and flour, and placed them in the oven. What a supper that was! We stayed and visited until a late hour, then piled into the wagon and went back home.

The boys had closed up both ends of their covered wagon and they slept there when it wasn't too cold. On the very cold nights they brought their bedrolls into the house and spread them on the floor. Beck, Don, and I slept in a "trundle bed."* There were only two rooms in the house—the big room, as we called it, and the kitchen. We ate our meals from a long table made of boards and two-by-fours. The folks' bed was also in the big room. It was made of boards and two-by-fours, a straw tick, and metal springs. There were some boxes and empty kegs for chairs.

The horses were usually all out in the pasture over the weekend, and when Pa wanted a team to drive, Glen and Ralph would go out into the pasture and chase them into the corral. On this morning the frost was white on the grass, with a cold north wind. The horses were frisky and took off for the corral at a dead run, bucking and kicking up their heels as they ran. Ralph came into the house. He had such a stricken look on his face that Ma knew at a glance there was something awfully wrong. "What in the world is the matter?" she asked Ralph.

---

*The trundle bed was built close to the floor with four casters under it. In the daytime it was trundled back under the big bed to be out of the way. I'm not sure they didn't "trunnel" (us kids' word for it) us back under there after we got to sleep.

Ralph's voice completely failed him on his first try, then he
said, "Barney b-b-b-broke his l-l-leg." Ralph's voice died away,
and his shoulders drooped as he stood heartbroken.

Pa turned to Glen. "What happened?"

"Barney slipped on the ice in the bogs as the horses came
off the hill. Some of them ran over him as he was tryin' to
get up."

"Are you sure his leg's broke?" Pa asked.

"Gotta be," Glen said. "Bone's stickin' out through the skin."

Pa looked slowly around the room at the stricken faces of
the family. Beck had thrown herself face down on the bed with
her arms locked around her head. Pa put on his cap and coat.
He picked the .30–30 from its hook on the wall. Out in the
corral, Barney had hobbled out of the bogs onto solid ground.
He nickered softly as Pa approached. Pa looked at him for a full
minute. "There's only one thing I can do, old pal. I wish there
was some other way, but there's not." He pulled back the hammer on the rifle, holding the muzzle an inch from Barney's
head. "It's just a short ways to the other shore," he said. But Pa
couldn't pull the trigger.

Us littlest kids couldn't remember when Barney wasn't in
the family. It just seemed like he had always been there, like
the rest of the brothers and sisters. Back to the house, Pa said
to Glen, "Go over and ask Adolph if he will come over. Tell
him to come right away if he can."

When they came back, Pa met Adolph at the kitchen door.
They talked in low tones for a while, then I heard Adolph say,
"Well, Bill, I ain't hankerin' for the job, but for you I'll do it."
Pa shut the door and stood leaning on the kitchen table. Don
and I held our hands over our ears. Adolph didn't come back
to the house after he finished his sorrowful task. He leaned the
.30–30 against the gate, took his team, and went on home.

Time passed slowly thereafter. We had a few light snows.
Some of the neighbors got together at Christmas. Ralph, Glen,

and Beck went to school, and Pa traveled around and bought a few horses. One day we got a chinook wind that melted off what little snow there was left. The wheat out south of the house looked fresh and green. We were seeing an occasional bunch of wild geese heading north. Spring was in the air.

Since Barney was gone, Pa told the boys they would have to pick out another horse and break him to the saddle. They talked it over between them for a week or so, then one Saturday morning they went out into the pasture and drove the horses into the corral. They had decided on the darkest of the two mares we had brought from Wyoming. Ralph got the lariat and tossed the loop over her head. She had been hitched to the wagon with old Bird several times, so she was broke to the bit. Us kids had made a sort of a pet of her. Ralph rode her around a while bareback, then they put the saddle on her and rode her around the place with the saddle most of the afternoon. That evening after supper we were all talking about the new saddle horse, so Ma said, "She's got to have a name. You're not goin' to just call her 'horse,' are you?"

We all picked out a name. Bessie said, "Call her Black Beauty!"

"She ain't black," Glen said, "she's chestnut."

"Chestnut Beauty is no good," Don said. "Why not just call her Beauty?"

"Whadda ya think we are, a bunch of sissies? She's got to have a name you can cuss at when you get mad," Ralph spoke up. "Sumthin' like Bell."

We couldn't agree on that either. Finally someone suggested we let Pa pick the name. After all, who knew more about horses than Pa? So we all agreed whatever Pa said would be her name. Pa was sitting at the pine board table with the lantern in front of him. He was writing some figures and names in a leather-backed daybook he always carried. He looked up from his work and, after a glance at each of us, he said, "Call her Laramie."

Several days later Pa came home leading a horse behind the wagon. "Figgered we'd need another saddle horse. He's already broke to ride and his name is Prince, so that's taken care of." Then to Ralph he said, "Get on him and try him out."

"That's a good-lookin' saddle and bridle," Ralph said. "Didja buy that too?"

"Yes, I did. I rode him some and the saddle felt real good, so I just bought the whole works."

We all stood around looking at the new horse. Ralph rode him down the road and back a couple times. "Seems to be well broke," he said, "and he has good speed, too." Then to Glen he said, "You can have Laramie. Prince is mine."

"Well, Bake,"* Pa said to Ma, "I sold the place. We'll be startin' for Howard County as soon as we can get the outfit ready." To Glen he said, "Saddle Laramie. I want you boys to ride them horses a lot in the next few days so you'll get used to each other. You've got a lot of ridin' to do between here and back home." We were all used to Pa's sudden decisions, so we didn't give that any concern. The main thing was we were going back home. In all our travels, before and after, the old homestead in Howard County was back home.

The next day Ralph started breaking Prince to work under the saddle while he used the big bullwhip. At first he just dragged the whip alongside, then, when Prince got used to that, he started swishing the whip out in front and across over Prince's head, making sure the whip never touched the horse. After a few days Prince lost his fear of the whip. Then Ralph started cracking the whip out to the sides, then gradually in front and to both sides, crossing over the horse's head and

---

*"Bake" was a pet name Pa had for Ma. He used to say bakin' bread was makin' love. "You can always tell what a woman thinks of her man by the bread she bakes for him."

back, making the whip crack like pistol shots at both ends of the arc.

"I'll race you to the main road," Glen said as he came alongside.

Ralph coiled up the big whip and said, "Let's go. With a sudden spurt Laramie was out ahead, but her lead didn't last long. Prince, with his long legs and rangy body, soon caught up and went out ahead.

The morning we left, several of the neighbors' families were there to see us off. George and Dellie came the night before and stayed all night. They brought bedclothes along and bedded most of their kids down on the floor while we shared the "trunnel bed" with another one or two. The Alan McMasters family, the Adolph Egleys, and the Lee Chalfant family were on hand bright and early. Everybody pitched in and helped get things ready to go. The boys had herded the horses into the corral the evening before and closed the gate. Some of the horses were broke to lead, and Pa had these tied behind our two wagons. Two horses behind each wagon, with the two wheel teams and the two saddle horses Ralph and Glen rode, made ten head under control. The rest of the herd (fifteen or twenty) were turned out into the yard and we were on our way. Pa took the driver's seat in the lead wagon and Ma held the lines on the team hitched to the second wagon. The neighbors had hitched their teams to their wagons, and they and the boys on their saddle horses formed a half circle around the herd and helped get them started. It was half a mile out to the main road, and when we got there, we headed east and the neighbors, all waving and calling good-bys, went their various ways to their homes.

Ralph and Glen had their hands full the rest of the day keeping the herd bunched around the wagons. Some of the more venturesome horses broke from the herd a few times but soon found themselves on the hot end of Ralph's big bullwhip. It takes a good horse, carrying a rider, to outrun an unmounted horse. Prince, however, proved to be equal to the job.

Pa had made arrangements to corral the horses the first night in the stockyards at Whitney. There was new grass along the road and the horses, after the first few miles, were more concerned with getting their fill of grass than exploring the countryside. We didn't stop for noon that first day, but kept going till we got to Whitney.

For some reason which I never could figure out, the stockyards at each little town were invariably located on the east side of town. The main road went through the center of town, or perhaps the towns sprang up on either side of the road. We took our herd of horses through town and corralled them in the stockyards. The wheel teams and the four led horses and the saddle horses were fed oats and hay. The rest had been cropping the new grass along the way, so they were pretty content. There was a windmill and water tank, and a good place to set up camp. While Ma and Beck were preparing supper, three men came down the road on foot from town. They stopped by the stock pens and looked the horses over for a while, then came on up to where Pa was leaning against a wagon wheel. They didn't look very prosperous, nor too clean, but that was not unusual for that country in 1907.

"Good-lookin' bunch of hosses you got there, stranger," one of the men said to Pa.

"Some of the best," Pa answered.

"Where you takin' 'em?"

"Down country."

"You ain't got much help for handlin' that many hosses."

"We get along."

"There ain't much you could do if somebody tried to run them off, is there?"

Pa walked over along the corral fence and picked up a

couple of whiskey bottles that had been tossed into the weeds. He came back and handed them to the man who had been doing most of the talking. He then went to the front of the wagon and pulled the .30–30 from its scabbard by the spring seat. Coming back to the men, he pulled the hammer back to full cock. "Throw them up," he said, "both at once, high!"

Pa had always referred to himself as half a man, him having only one arm, and being lame in one leg from a bout with polio and short of breath from the asthma, so he said he had to put up a good bluff. In my seven-year-old mind, I used to wonder what Pa would do if somebody called his bluff sometime.

The man leaned forward, then, snapping erect, he threw the bottles high into the air. The little .30–30 roared and the first bottle exploded on the way up. Then, with that little one-handed flip of his, Pa threw another shell into the chamber, and as the stock touched his shoulder the gun roared again and the second bottle flew to bits at the top of its climb into the air. The glass rained down around the men's heads as the smoke from the gun drifted lazily down the slight breeze. Pa tucked the stock of the .30–30 between his elbow and ribs. He looked steadily at the men for a full minute. "Does that answer your question?"

The next morning after breakfast, Pa told Glen to saddle Laramie. To Ma he said, "I'm goin' up town. Have the boys hitch up and get ready to go. I'll be back in a short while." We all busied ourselves with our usual duties, kidding and scolding one another as we went about our work. We had everything ready to roll when Pa got back. He dismounted and put a package in the wagon. We were all curious to know what was in the package, but we would never ask, as we knew Pa would let us know when he was ready.

A short distance away from town we were in good grass and

the herd, being shut in all night, busied themselves with getting their fill as we moved slowly along. The boys kept them bunched up in a loose formation behind and to either side of the wagons. The road angled off to the southeast and by late noon we got into rough, rocky country, with some brush and scattered pine trees. We stopped for our midday meal along a little creek where the horses could get a drink.

After we had eaten our lunch, Pa went to the wagon and got the package. He picked out a flat rock and sat on it. He spread the wrappings out on the ground and laid out a shell belt, two boxes of cartridges, an armpit holster, and a shiny blue .38 Colt automatic pistol. "Beansie," he said to me, "open a box of them shells and fill all them loops in that belt." I was proud to be given such an important task. Those bright, shiny cartridges looked so beautiful to me that their deadly significance never entered my mind. Ma and Ralph fitted the holster over Pa's shoulder and adjusted the straps across his back. He put the pistol in the holster and moved around a bit to get the feel of it. He drew the gun from the holster a couple of times. It didn't come out very easy. "Well, there's one thing sure, the damn thing ain't gonna *fall* out!"

He picked the shell belt up by the big buckle and gave it a flip around his waist. Catching the strap end between his two first fingers, with his thumb back of the buckle, he deftly

This is one of the first of the automatic pistols made by Colt. The hammer did not have a cocking spur. It was rounded over the top and knurled to keep the thumb from slipping off. It had a six-inch barrel, and held ten cartridges. It felt muzzle heavy to hold in your hand, but it was deadly accurate.

slipped the strap through and fastened it loosely around his waist. He removed the clip from the butt of the pistol without taking the gun from the holster. Holding the clip against the holster with his stub arm, he filled it with shells from the belt, then pushed it back into the gun. To Ralph he said, "You boys mount up and watch the horses. I'm goin' down the creek a ways and get the feel of this gun." To me he said, "Come on, Beansie, lets go."

We went down through some timber around a bend in the creek where the sound of the shots would be muffled from the horses. "Gather up ten or a dozen of those rocks," he said to me, "and set them in a row on the creek bank."

"How big rocks, Pa?"

"Oh, size of a muskmelon or so."

The rocks were mostly chunks that had crumbled from a limestone stratum which protruded from the slope of the hill. I set them about a foot apart and came back to where Pa stood. "Now you stand back behind me," Pa told me. "We don't know where this thing is goin' to shoot."*

To load the first shell into the chamber of an automatic pistol, the gun must be held by the butt and the slide pulled back as far as it will go, then let snap forward. This moves the first load into firing position. The first shot automatically reloads, and the pistol is ready to fire again. Loading the first shell into the chamber was giving Pa some trouble, it being a two-handed operation.

"Can't I help you Pa?" I asked.

"No, I've got to learn to do it myself. I might have to sometime when you are not around." He placed the butt of the pistol under his stub arm, with the muzzle pointing downward, then with his one hand worked the slide. The gun was

---

*Handgun shooting was not new to Pa, although he had been without one for a couple of years. The one he had before was a .44 Smith and Wesson single-action. He gave it to my brother Walt for helping pick corn.

now ready to fire. It was a very dangerous procedure. To Pa it was a carefully considered risk.

He took careful aim at the first rock on the left and pulled the trigger. The rock exploded into a pile of rubble. Pa lowered the gun a bit and stood looking thoughtfully down at it. It was all ready to shoot, just as before. Then, raising it again, he took the next nine rocks at about one-second intervals. The gun was empty and there was only rubble where the rocks had been. Pa turned to me. "What a wicked machine," he said. "I hope I never have to use it on anything but rocks."

We made it to the McPherson ranch by early dusk that evening, and with the horses all shut safely in the ranch corral we spent a restful night.

The next day, a little before noon, it started to rain, so we didn't stop for noon but kept moving along. "There'll be times like this aplenty before we get home," Pa told us. We ate snacks of whatever we could find in the grub box. Pa changed places with Ralph while Ralph got something to eat, and after Ralph got back on Prince, Glen tied Laramie to the back of Ma's wagon and let her follow while he got into the wagon and ate some lunch. Both boys had "duckin" coats, which were nearly waterproof, and their old felt hats kept the water from running down their necks.*

A few days later we reached Alliance, where we spent the night, and as usual Pa got permission to corral the horses in the stockyards east of town. The next morning Pa told Ralph and Glen to stay with the horses. The rest of us took the wagons and went uptown. At the general store Pa bought supplies for the next couple of hundred miles. He got a lot of good eats and some treats. When the stuff was all in the wagons there wasn't much room for us kids.

---

*"Duckin' coats," made of heavy duck cloth similar to tent material, usually had large pockets and sometimes a game-carrying pocket in the back which was often used while duck hunting.

Back on the trail again, with a nice spring breeze and plenty of grass for the horses, who by this time required very little herding, everybody was filled with happy thoughts of getting home again. The four horses we had led behind the wagons at first were turned loose with the rest, so they could eat grass as we went along. We could hear the boys whistling and could occasionally catch the strains of "Buffalo Gals" from Ralph's mouth harp. I was riding on the spring seat in the lead wagon with Pa. Ma, Beck, and Don were in the second wagon. The horses, with plenty of good grass, were filling out in fine shape. Pa sang a few bars of "Barbry Allen," then he turned and looked at me. "Well, Beansie, it's all downhill from here on."

《》

McKee's Mill

《》

On February 22, 1908, a late snowstorm dumped four inches of soft, wet snow on the ground. It came down so quietly none of us knew about it until morning. At breakfast, Pa wondered if it would hurt our sale. We had about forty horses, a little household stuff, some haying tools, and the covered wagons posted on sale bills, and were looking forward to the rewards for spending most of a year gathering the herd over Wyoming and Nebraska. Horses were in big demand here in Howard County, and all of the farming country for that matter.

About ten o'clock the wagons and other rigs began arriving. The clouds broke up, and as the sun came out the snow became slushy and was soon soaking into the ground. There was free lunch at noon, and some of the neighbor women, along with my older sisters, Em and Jose, fixed big loads of sandwiches and coffee.

Pa and my brothers Ralph and Glen had spent the previous summer and winter breaking horses and matching teams. The weather had been favorable for grass, and with some corn and oats and hay the horses were in fine shape. The bidding was spirited, and some of the poor-looking colts that Pa had bought for $10 to $25 brought $100 or more. One team of jet black driving horses sold to Oliver Starkey for over $500, and that represented a lot of value in that spring of 1908.

As the sun sank behind a rim of new clouds in the west, the last of the crowd had taken their purchases and gone their way. Pa came into the house tired, and wet from the melting snow. "I'll ride to town with Dick and Em in the morning and get the figures straightened up."

Within a week we—Pa, Ma, Ralph, Glen, Beck, Don, and I—were aboard the CB&Q emigrant train headed for Medford, Oregon. Ma and Jose and Em (my older sisters who, like Walt and Dellie, had left the family circle even before the trip to Thermopolis) had fried chickens and packed a large basket of sandwiches and other kinds of food to eat on the long trip. Pa's asthma had not improved, and he was still looking for a place where he could breathe easier. Lee Herron, an old crony of his, told him to get into the pine forests where he could breathe the ozone.

At Spokane we spent the night on a siding without heat, while our wheezy old engine went into the shop for repairs. It was a chilly night, and we huddled together with all our coats spread over us.

From there we went to Seattle, and then south across Washington, crossing the Columbia estuary on a ferryboat. The novelty had long since worn off train travel and we were looking forward to our journey's end. Compared with travel by emigrant train, we all agreed, the covered wagons were to be preferred.

Back in St. Paul, Pa had become acquainted with George Iams, who was a younger brother of Frank Iams, the noted horse importer and breeder. George had worked for his brother, Frank, for some time, but they were too much alike to stay together, both being hot-headed. Their differences ended in a fight, and George left St. Paul and went to Medford, Oregon. Later he wrote to Pa telling what a fine country Oregon was: lots of fruit, warm summers, miles and miles of pine forests, and cheap land. So it was that Pa had decided upon Medford as his next home.

Our old train puffed its way into Medford in midmorning and rolled to a stop with a big sigh of escaping steam. It seemed to settle down on its axles and doze. The baggage smashers, as Pa called them, dumped our belongings out on the platform. Besides our old trunk there were a couple of large wooden boxes, all tied securely with many feet of strong rope. We all gathered around the boxes, glad to be out of the dirty old rail coach at last. "Stay here with the stuff," Pa said, "while I hunt up a dray team."

He returned in about an hour with some crackers and cheese and some fruit and candy. "The drayman won't be here until after dinner," he said, "so we might as well eat." Ma put what was left of our lunch out on one of the boxes and opened the crackers and cheese and other stuff. How delicious that fresh food was! It disappeared like magic.

After a while, a team hitched to a light wagon stopped at the platform, and the drayman and Ralph and Glen loaded the trunk and boxes aboard. Ma and Don rode up on the spring seat with the driver. The rest of us sat or stood around the boxes. Pa gave the address where we wanted to go.

The George Iams family consisted of the parents, a daughter about seven, and a son about five, maybe six. The girl's name was Hazel. She was dark like her father and good-looking like her mother. The boy's name was Raymond; he was slightly undersized for his age and much like his sister in looks. The Iamses seemed genuinely glad to see us, although back in St. Paul the two families (except for Pa and George) were scarcely acquainted. We all felt ill at ease in their nice home. The long train ride had left us dust-covered and streaked with soot from the coal smoke, which seeped into the old rail coach through countless cracks and openings left by missing ventilation panes.

Pa and us boys washed our hands and faces in a wash basin on the back porch while Ma and Beck cleaned up somewhere in the house. After supper Ma filled a sack with clean clothes and handed it to Ralph. "There's soap and towels in there," she said. "Use it." George and Pa led the way, and a few blocks east we came to a footpath leading down through high bushes to the Bear River. "There's a swimmin' hole downstream a short ways," George told the boys. "The water is a little cool yet, but after your long train ride I think you will enjoy it."

We spent the night in the Iamses' home, bedded down in our own bedding, which Ma and Ralph unpacked from the big wooden box. We spread our quilts on the living room floor and we all slept like logs. The next morning George said to us kids, "Well, how did you like sleeping on the floor?" Glen, who was never very generous with his compliments, answered, "I've sure slept in a helluva lot worse places!" George got a big laugh out of that.

After breakfast Pa and George left the house, and the rest of us sat around or walked up and down the street. In about an hour they returned with the dray wagon. Pa explained that they had found a place where we could camp, in the backyard of one of George's friends, whose land ran down to the river-bank.

The Bear River at that point made a little oxbow covered with green grass and wildflowers. We set up our tent and unpacked what we needed for the time being. The front of our tent faced the east and was about a dozen paces from the edge of the water. The river was from six to a dozen feet wide and averaged a foot or more deep. The water was clear and ran over pebbles and rocks. Upriver and down from our little oxbow was brush and trees. "We will stay here until I can find us a place to move into," Pa said. "It may take a while to find what I want." Well, it did take a while—two weeks to be exact.

There was a narrow-gauge railroad from Medford to Jacksonville, a distance of eight or nine miles. The little train had a wood-burning engine and it had to stop halfway through the run to take on fuel. Jacksonville was only a village, but it was older than Medford and was still the county seat. After contacting different real estate men in Medford without finding what he wanted, Pa took the little train to the county seat and, with the help of the county clerk, searched through the records until he found something interesting. "How about this McKee's Mill?" he asked the clerk.

After looking up the details, the clerk said, "There's a couple years' back taxes on it. It's listed as 280 acres of timber and old buildings and a sawmill that has been out of operation for a long time. It's about fourteen miles southeast of here, pretty rough country. Also there's a store and post office called Ruch (it's pronounced Roosh) a mile or two from the mill. There's a stage road from here up through Ruch and on up to Blue Ledge." Pa spent the night in Jacksonville and went by stage to Ruch the next day.

Back in our camp on the Bear River, us kids were getting acquainted with the surrounding area. We waded in the river and fished and did other things kids do. One day a bearded young man came to our camp. He talked to Ma a while at the tent, then went over to the river where the boys were fishing.

"Having any luck?" he asked.

"Not much," they answered. "Seems like the fish are so scary we can't get close enough to them so they can see our bait."

"Them's trout. They are shy. I can't catch them either. Come back over to your tent and ask your mamma for a little piece of bread and I'll show you how we fish over in the Jungle." The Jungle was a hobo camp over on the other side of the bridge. We had seen the light from their campfires on a few occasions.

Glen went into the tent and found a piece of bread. The young hobo took a short stick from his pocket and unrolled a length of fishline—it had a hook and sinker much like any fishline. He took the bread and moistened it in his mouth, then rolled it into a hard little ball and molded it around the hook. "Now," he said, "you kids stay back and keep still." Swinging the bait around his head a couple of times, he threw it out towards where the chickens were scratching. Our camp was only a short distance from the house where the owner of our campsite lived, and their chickens were around our camp most every day. A hen picked up the bait and the young man jerked the line much as you would "strike a fish." He pulled the line in, hand over hand. The hen, with the ball of dough and hook in her throat, didn't even let out a squawk.

Ma came out of the tent in time to see him pick up the chicken. "Young man, if I'd known you were going to do that, I wouldn't have given you the bread. Don't you know that's stealing?"

"Sorry, ma'am," the young man said, "but when you're as hungry as I am, you get your chicken first then pray for forgiveness." He tucked the hen under his arm and said, "There will be chicken stew in the Jungle tonight."

Ma looked at us kids with a thoughtful expression on her face. "Your pa never did anything like that." Then, with a twinkle in her eyes, "But he is an expert with that hickory cane of his."

The road from Jacksonville to Ruch was surfaced in some places with crushed rock from the rock quarry at Quarry Hill. The material was similar to Sherman Hill rock in Wyoming, but was gray instead of red brown. There were some pretty steep grades going towards Ruch from Jacksonville, especially coming down into the valley from Quarry Hill. The stage was not the regular stagecoach type, but was more like the rig back in Nebraska that we called a spring wagon. It had three seats and a flat top with side curtains that could be pulled down in rainy weather. It was pulled by four mules that maintained a good, steady trot, except on the steepest hills. The people called it a hack.

Pa got off the hack at Ruch and went into the store. A man sat tilted back in a chair with his feet up on a packing box. He looked up when Pa came in but didn't move. Pa sat on a nail keg nearby and didn't say anything while the man studied him from head to foot. Finally he asked Pa, "You want something?"

"I'm looking for a man named Cap Ruch," Pa said.

"You've found him," the man said. "What can I do for you?"

"My name is Bill Scott. I'm from the east. I've come out here for my health. I would like to buy a place out here somewheres to make my home. Could you tell me how to find a place called McKee's Mill?"

After some hesitation and a further searching look at Pa, he said, "Call me Cap; everybody else does." He got up and motioned Pa to follow. Out on the store platform he pointed to a rutted wagon road leading up the slope. "It's up there a mile or so."

Pa looked at the road. "It don't look like it has been used much. Anybody live up there?"

"Yeah," Cap answered. "What's left of 'em." He turned and studied Pa again for a while, then said, "Thur's a foot trail takes off from the road a couple jumps up the slope. Take that; it's easier climbin' than the road." He turned then and went back into the store.

Pa decided he would eat a bite before he started up through the timber. He went back into the store. "I'd like to buy some cheese and crackers to take along," he said.

Cap cut off a hunk of cheese from a big round block of longhorn and picked up a big handful of crackers from a barrel just inside the counter. He laid them on a paper on the counter. "Eat it here if you want," he said. Then he went into the back room of the store, where he had his living quarters.

Pa was about through with his cheese and crackers and was glancing around for a water pail when Cap came from the back room with a big cup of steaming coffee. He set the cup in front of Pa and went back into the back room without saying anything.

Pa finished his lunch and went to the door leading to the bachelor quarters. "How much?" he asked, pulling his purse from his pocket.

"On the store," Cap said with a short wave of his hand. "Y'er welcome."

Pa spent an hour or more on the short trail to the McKee front gate. A part rail and part stake and rider fence enclosed the entire farmstead. Inside of that there was a picket fence enclosing the house and garden.

Pa made his way to the yard gate and lifted the latch and stepped inside the yard. A very large dog got up from a mat on the porch and began to bark. A gray-haired woman came out of the house and wound her fingers in the deep fur on the back of the dog's neck. "Now, Laddie," she told the huge dog, "come back and lay down. Come on up, mister," she said to Pa. "Laddie knows you are a friend." At the bottom of the steps Pa stopped and explained that he was from the east, and was looking for a place in the pine forest.

It was typical of Pa to finish a deal once he had started it, so we were not surprised when he came driving into our camp with a team and wagon. He had been gone from Medford for several days, and there was no way to communicate from out in the hills. Of course, the first thing we all wanted to know was "Did you get us a place to live?"

"Unhitch the team and give them some feed and water," Pa told the boys. "I'll tell you all about it after I've had some supper." Pa seemed well pleased and said that he had not had a bad wheezing spell since he left our camp.

After supper Pa began. "I bought a place way back in the

piney woods. The old couple that lived there were having a hard time making a go of it. Neither of them were able to work much, and their two boys had left home to find jobs of their own. They were anxious to sell, so I bought the whole shebang, except their clothes and quilts and stuff. I helped them pack up and brought them to Jacksonville, where we stopped at the courthouse and finished up the deal. They have some relatives in Jacksonville and are staying with them until they find themselves a house."

"What's the place like, Pa?" we all wanted to know. "You'll soon find out," Pa said. "We'll be on our way there early tomorrow. Sam McKee said to get back as soon as we could, because the pack rats were real bad thereabouts."

The next morning our camp just sort of melted away. We were old hands at breaking camp, and we were packed and ready to go before the sun had cleared the hogback east of the valley. Pa went up to the house where the people lived and offered to pay them for the use of their backyard. The lady said, "No. We enjoyed your visit. Your missus and I had several long visits while you folks were here. She told me all about the east. I do hope you and your little crippled boy feel better here."

We said good-by to the George Iams family and thanked them for their help. "Come out and see us," Ma said to Mrs. Iams. "I'll probably get pretty lonesome way back out in the mountains."

The stage road from Medford across the valley had a crushed rock surface. The soil in the valley was deep and black. An almond grove a ways from town was in early bloom, the pink blossoms and tiny new leaves making a beautiful sight. At Jacksonville we took the blue lead road and after climbing the long, steep Quarry Hill, Pa stopped the team and let them rest. The team was a horse and a mule. The mule was a jenny. Pa said the McKees named her Maud after the funny-paper mule in "Happy Hooligan," because she was full of tricks.

The mountains were not exactly new to any of us, because we had seen mountains before in Wyoming. These were different, however, in the fact that they were mostly covered with pine forests on both sides of the Applegate valley. Pa had bought some supplies in Medford, but he stopped at Ruch and bought quite a bit more stuff that he happened to remember we needed.

A big, tall pine tree stood by the main gate to the farmstead. The gate was made of rough sawed pine boards like most all the other buildings on the place. A partly built barn, however, was made of logs, but was built only up to the top of the walls, with no roof. The house was built of rough sawed boards and roofed with "shakes." There was no paint on anything, and the place had the appearance of being very old.

Pa stopped the team at the front gate. "Glen," he said, "unhitch the team and put them in the barn. The rest of us will start moving in." Laddie, the big dog, came down to the gate to greet us, having recognized the team and remembered Pa. By nightfall we had all our belongings carried in and fires built in the big fireplace and the kitchen range. The fireplace was very big and was made of bricks. It had a big iron hook on each side (called cranes) and a big black iron kettle hanging on each hook. These cranes could be swung in or out of the fire as needed for cooking or serving.

After supper we all sat around the big fireplace talking about the house. There was a loft with a stairway on the outside leading up into it. That was to be the bedroom for us boys, except Don, who seemed to be walking more painfully as the time went by. There was an old velvet-covered couch, with horsehair stuffing showing through in places, in the living room, and Don claimed that for his bed. The front bedroom was for Ma and Pa and a tiny room off the kitchen was for Bessie (Beck). Laddie, the dog, joined the circle before the fireplace. He had his spot, and he lay down there. He always lay in the same place, just to one side of the big rock slab which made the hearth.

The kitchen had a range stove and a long work bench along the east wall. The dining table was in the kitchen. There was a long hallway clear through the house from west to east, with an outside door at each end. The kitchen door and the living room door opened off this hallway, opposite each other. Most of the furniture had been made there in the shop. The chairs were turned on the shop lathe and set together with linchpins. The seats were woven from strips cut from thongs out of natural deer hides, with the hair still on. There were straw ticks on the beds.

The back porch rested on the ground. As the slope tilted sharply to the west, the front porch was built up on posts. The stairs to the loft were on the outside of the house, next to the garden.

All the pots, pans, dishes, tools, and everything but the McKees' quilts and clothing were just as they had been when the McKees were there. The upstairs, or loft, as we called it, was not finished inside, and in dry weather the shakes (homemade shingles) would shrink and let the stars shine through in

places. During the rainy season, the cracks would close up and keep out most of the rain.

There was a short length of chain wired to the back door that was hooked over a spike when we wanted the door held shut. There were no screens on the doors or windows, as the few flies present in that high valley were kept under control by the green wood lizards which scuttled to and fro most everywhere. These little serpents were six or eight inches long, green on their backs, and a mottled gray brown on their sides and underneath. They were harmless and very quick and cunning. They could hide before your eyes on a moldy log or board and blend with the background. We were a little skittish about them at first but soon learned to live with them.

Along in the night, after the fire had burned low in the fireplace on our first night there, Ma heard Don call from the living room. "Ma," he said "I can't sleep. There's something itching me all over. Won't you come see what's the matter?"

Ma lit the lamp and turned the covers back from Don's couch. "Good heavens," she said, "you're covered with bedbugs! Pa," she called, "come here and look." After some discussion they decided to put Don at the foot of their bed until morning. After many months of camping out and sleeping under all kinds of conditions, we didn't panic over a few bedbugs. Next morning at breakfast we were all scratching a bit here and there, but still anxious to get out and look over our new surroundings.

The backyard was bare of grass, and was mostly gumbo clay and rocks. While us kids were out looking over the scenery, Pa had ripped a corner of the velvet cover from Don's couch. "Ralph! Glen!" he called from the back door. "Come carry this old couch out in the backyard." That done, he proceeded to saturate the sides and ends with coal oil (kerosene). He then made a torch from a dry pine bough and, walking around the old couch, he set fire all around the outer edge. We stood, fascinated, as we watched the bed bugs start moving to the center, away from the fire. The top of the couch soon became one solid mat of writhing, crawling bugs. We could hear popping sounds as they exploded like popcorn. The stench of burning horse hair and frying bugs soon drove us back a distance. Pa said, "I'll bet some of them old boys have been living in that since Lewis and Clark came through." Ma had made a tour of inspection about the house, and she soon had all hands busy with scrub brushes or rags saturated with coal oil and lye soap suds, in a concerted clean-up campaign.

There were some chickens scratching around the yard, mostly brown Leghorns and some mixtures. Just to the southeast corner of the house was a quite large building made of home-sawed lumber like the rest. This, Sam McKee explained to Pa before they left, was the storehouse. During the summer they hauled dry wood and stored it for winter, when the rain kept everything soaked for months. There were also supposed to be some hogs with the place. We were to meet them later.

Laddie, our dog, came with the farm. He was black, with a white vest and blaze face. He was very big, and friendly with us kids. He was so big, in fact, that at first we thought we could ride on his back. He soon gave us to understand he was not a horse.

There were some old guns and reloading tools, and down in the shop, which was at the west edge of the barnyard, there were a forge, anvil, vise, and hand tools, all very old and worn. Also, there was a wood-turning lathe run by a treadmill.

The canal, which carried the water from the reservoir to the sawmill, appeared to climb up the side of the mountain on the other side of the creek. Us kids couldn't understand how water could run up the side of the mountain. The old sawmill itself had long since been sold and carted away. Only the canal and the old rusty pipe were left. There were some prospecting tools and a box of dynamite caps, along with some double-bit

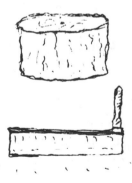

Laddie (Ol' Lad)
He would rather hunt than eat!

axes, a foot adze, and a shingle-making outfit consisting of a shake froe and maul. To make shakes, one man placed the blade at the exact thickness wanted on the end of the block and held it upright while the other man swung the maul. The slabs split off could be anywhere from thirty inches to four feet long, depending upon what kind of building they were used for.

Block of
straight-grained pine

Shake Froe

Maul
Block of hardwood
with iron bands

There was a building near the barn where hay was stacked for winter use. It was a simple $\wedge$ shaped roof covered with shakes, and open at both ends.

Along in the afternoon of that first day after we arrived at the mill we saw a woman coming down the path from up the slope to the east. "Looks like we've got company," Pa said. "I heard there was a family living up near the reservoir."

The woman came through the backyard gate and up to the kitchen porch. "Howdy, neighbors," she said. "I hear tell yore from the east. I jist thought I'd come down and welcome you to yore new home." She turned to Ma and handed her a quart jar about half full of some slimy-looking stuff. "I brought you some sourdough starter. I knowed you wouldn't have any after comin' so fur."

Ma thanked her and said we were glad we had some neighbors.

"My name is Miry Thurman," she said. "My first husband's name was Morgan. He was a second cousin of J. P. Morgan. My two kids' name is Morgan, so you can see we come from a snooty fambly. But jus' call me Miry. What's yore name, missus?"

"My name is Lizzie," Ma answered, "and (pointing to Pa) that's my husband, Bill Scott."

"Hi, Bill," Miry said, shaking hands with Pa. "Whut happened to your other arm? I see you ain't got nuthin' in yer sleeve but a knot."

"Got it shot off durin' the Injun wars," Pa answered with a straight face, "an I ain't never liked Injuns since."

"I used to live here when I was a girl," Miry said, "but after I married Morgan and moved away, old McKee got holt of the place somehow."

After Pa quit smoking a pipe on our trip to Wyoming he went quite a while without using tobacco, but later on he started using a little chewing tobacco. Now he got out his plug

of horseshoe and nibbled off a corner of the plug. Miry's eyes
lighted up. "Bill," she said, "yer just the man I'm lookin' fer.
Hows about a bite offen that plug of horseshoe?"

Pa handed her the plug, and after biting off a chunk she

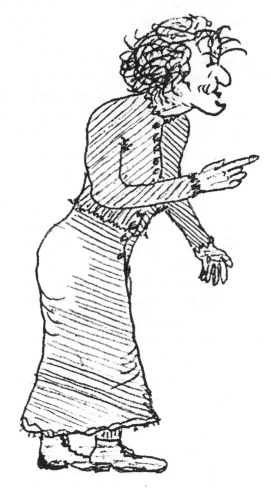

Plug of chewing
tobacco with
horseshoe emblem

Miry Thurman
(Catamount)

chewed on it a bit. Then, turning her head, she squirted a stream of tobacco juice at a rock a dozen feet away, hitting it dead center. She turned and winked at Pa, then to Ma she said, "Lizzie, do ya s'pose you could lend me a haffa cuppa sugar? Charley, that's my man, he's workin' at the blacksmith shop down at Ruch. Soon as he gits his pay, I'll pay ya back."

We soon met the rest of the Thurman family, Perry, a gangling fourteen-year-old boy, and his sister, a couple of years younger. She was a blonde with a light complexion and untidy appearance. In fact, most everybody around had sort of an untidy appearance, including the Scott family.

It was coming on summer, and Pa kept us boys busy getting things organized. First we hauled rocks from the field and piled them around the edge, and repaired the rail fence. The country was free range and livestock had to be fenced out of the fields where they were not wanted. The field was some ten acres in size, and was surrounded in all directions with thick timber, except for the lane to get into the field. A gate is not needed in a rail fence, because the rails can be let down anywhere and laid back up in a few minutes.

We thought we had picked up all the rocks, but when Ralph plowed the field a new crop of rocks appeared. After the oats were sown and harrowed in, Pa told the boys they could have some time to go hunting, so Ralph got out the 12-gauge and Glen took a little .22 rifle that had been left in the house. As soon as they got the guns, Laddie, who by now had become "Old Lad" to all of us, began to dance around and bark with joy.

Pa took the team and wagon, and with me up on the spring seat beside him, we left the place and headed down toward Ruch. Ruch was also the local post office. The mail was brought from Jacksonville by hack twice a week. We tied the team to the hitch rack and went into the store. Pa spoke to the storekeeper. "Mornin' Cap."

"Mornin, Bill," Cap answered. "What can I do for you?"

"I'll need a box of .22 rifle shells, a plug of horseshoe, and fifty pounds of beans and some information." Cap set the articles on the counter, then stood looking at Pa. "Anybody around here keep cattle?"

"Yeah," Cap answered, "Some of the farmers down the valley's got 'em. There's Buckleys and Van Dervort not far down the river, and Kaufmans over a little further west." Pa paid for his purchases, and as Cap seemed to want to say something more, Pa waited. Cap looked intently at Pa for a while, then asked, "Met yer neighbor up the creek yet?"

"Yes," Pa answered, "the whole family been down to see us several times."

Cap was having a hard time saying these words, but they finally came out. "Bill, you're an honest man, but that don't mean everybody up that creek is. Charley has made his brag that 'I'll have that old eastern tenderfoot run out inside of a year.' " The two men stood looking at each other for some time. Then, being sure they understood each other, Pa nodded his head and picked up the sack of beans. I put the .22 shells and the plug of horseshoe in my pockets and we went out to the wagon.

Following the stage road downriver for a ways, Pa finally spoke, "We'll try the Buckleys first. At the Buckley farm we tied the team to the hitching post and went up the path toward the well-kept farmhouse. A couple of dogs came trotting down the path with wagging tails, barking to announce our presence. A middle-aged lady came to the door and called the dogs back. Pa took off his Stetson and held it in his hand. "Mornin', ma'am," he said. "Could I speak to your husband?"

"Sure," she said. "He's over at the barn. Just go on over and holler 'John.' You'll find him."

We located John, and as he and Pa shook hands, John said, "You must be the man that moved on the old McKee place."

After some visiting and getting acquainted, Pa said, "I'm looking for a cow that's giving milk. Cap Ruch said you might have one you would sell. There's seven of us in the family, and we need milk. I'd like to get a gentle cow that the missus can milk." Then, with a grin, "You see, I've just got one hand, and I expect my boys will be huntin' squirrels sometimes when milkin' time comes."

John 'lowed he could spare a cow for a neighbor, and he and Pa walked out among the cows in the lot. They came back through the barn, and John hollered up to the house. As his wife came to the door, he called, "Company for dinner."

"I figgered as much," she answered.

John turned to Pa. "C'mon up to the house and visit a while. We can't dicker on an empty stummick anyhow."

We reached home about sundown that evening, leading the cow behind the wagon. She hadn't been much trouble to lead, as she was used to being tied up at milking time. We stopped the team to let her rest frequently, so she stood the trip real well. She was fair-sized as Jerseys go, with a shiny black back and some brindle down her sides, blending to tan and cream color under her belly. She had beautifully curved horns with points right out in front, and soft velvety brown eyes.

As the days and weeks wore into summer and the hot sun turned everything into a tinderbox, Pa often cautioned all of us to be extra careful with fire. With the Fourth of July coming up, he was fearful of fireworks setting off a forest fire. "You'll have to get along with cap pistols this year," he told us.

We had all been busy. Pa and us boys finished the barn and covered it with shakes that we had made ourselves. We had built a rock wall around the spring where we got our drinking water, and put a roof over it supported by four stout posts. When the rock wall filled up to the overflow, we had a stream of sparkling cold water to hold our water bucket under, instead of having to dip it out of the spring, which was in the edge of the creek.

The Thurman family had often been visitors in the days and weeks past, Perry and Annie Morgan eating many noontime meals with us. They didn't have anything to do at home, so they spent a lot of time at our place playing with whatever of us kids weren't busy.

The warm, dry days and pure air up in that high little valley seemed to agree with Pa and he had not had any bad wheezing spells for some weeks. The opposite was true with Don. By now he could not walk without crutches, and even then it was so painful he spent most of his time sitting in his little rocking chair, propped up with cushions.

The young gray squirrels were almost full-grown, and we often had oven-roasted squirrel, with sliced onions and gravy. Old Lad loved to hunt squirrels. Us boys, or, more often, Ralph and Glen, would go off into the woods and Old Lad would run on ahead until he would get on track of a squirrel. He would chase it up a tree and then he would sit under the tree and bark until the boys would come and shoot the squirrel. He had a certain bark he used, and as Ralph described it, "When Old Lad barks treed, you can be sure he's got a squirrel up there."

Soon after we got our cow we decided to name her Silk because of her shiny coat. She didn't give a lot of milk, but Jersey milk is rich, and we often had cream for our blackberries and cherries. Silk roamed the orchard to graze. There was lush grass and a legume called filaree there. One time, someone of the family sent Old Lad up into the orchard to bring Silk down to the barn at milking time, with almost disastrous results. Old Lad grabbed her by the hind leg and sat back on his haunches to hold. In her panic, Silk whirled and lost her footing. She rolled over on her back and Old Lad kept her leg stretched out so she couldn't get up. Silk's terrified bawling brought Ralph and Glen on the run to make Old Lad let loose. Silk was so frightened she held up her milk that evening. Sam McKee had told Pa that Laddie was trained to catch animals and hold them until his owner came, but Pa had forgotten all about it until then.

One morning, a week or so later, as we headed into fall, Pa had put Ralph and Glen to cutting stove wood and piling it in ricks and called me to come with him. It was early in the forenoon, and at that altitude the cool of night had not left our little valley. We hitched Dick and Maud to the wagon and I opened the big gate. "Get in," Pa said, "I'm going to the store for some supplies and you can carry them out to the wagon for me."

This was on a Saturday, and down at the store several lumberjacks were making their purchases. Then they would sit out on the porch to visit. As we came down our road and across the little flat stretch to the store, one of the men said, "Well, look what's comin' out of the bushes! Must be the old tenderfoot Charley told us about." They watched with interest as Pa drove up to the hitch rack. One fellow had a big white bulldog sitting by his feet. He nudged the man next to him. "Looks like he's got his dog along! Maybe we can have some fun."

Pa handed me the lines to hold while he nodded to the men on the porch. "Howdy," he said, "nice mornin'."

Some of the men nodded while others just sat and watched. "That yore dog?" the man with the bulldog asked Pa.

"I reckon he's mine all right," Pa answered. "Why?"

"I'll betcha two bits my dog can lick 'im," the man said.

"I don't think my dog wants to fight," Pa said, looking down at Old Lad, who stood by the wagon with his tail waving back and forth.

The lumberjack squirted a stream of tobacco juice into the gravel. "Let's let the dogs decide that," he said. "Go git 'im, Rex!"

Rex came charging toward the wagon, growling his challenge. He slammed his big, muscular chest against Laddie's shoulder, expecting him to go rolling on the ground. Laddie didn't roll; he just sort of hunched his shoulder forward to meet the charge. The bulldog roared his rage and sank his teeth into the deep, curly fur on the side of Laddie's neck. So far, Old Lad had not made a single aggressive move. Rex, taking this to mean an easy victory, braced his feet and reared back to give his victim the shaking that usually ended the fight. Instead of pulling back, Laddie moved quickly forward, which caused the bulldog's front feet to be exposed in a spraddled position. Old Lad grabbed one of those feet in his big jaws and shut down. I could hear the crunch of bones even above the noise of the battle. The bulldog made another try to shake his opponent, but the pain in his foot was becoming so great his rage ended in a howl of pain. He whirled to get away and found himself flipped neatly on his back, with Old Lad still holding his foot and grinding the bones.

The surprising turn of events brought some of the men to their feet, to better watch the contest. The bulldog's owner grabbed a rock from the ground and started toward the dogs, but the men took the rock from his hand and pushed him back down on the porch. He yelled at Pa, "Call yer dog off. He's gonna cripple my dog for life." Pa took his tobacco from his pocket and bit off a chew. He chewed thoughtfully for a few moments, then he aimed a stream of tobacco juice at Old Lad's nose and cut loose. The result was surprisingly sudden. Old Lad loosed his hold and backed away. The bulldog got to his feet and hobbled away, still howling with pain. With his owner walking beside him, they went off into the woods.

We tied the team to the hitch rack and went up the steps to the store. The men stood aside for us to go in. Some of the men had grins on their faces. In the store, Cap Ruch handed Pa a plug of horseshoe. "My compliments," he said. "What can I do for you today?"

There was wind over the mountain tops and we could see clouds moving up the slopes at times, but the wind never blew down in our valley. As we headed into fall, the manzanita berries colored the slopes and the pears and apples began to ripen. The acorns had not started to drop yet, but there was a scattering of apples and pears under the trees. The oat crop was cut for hay and stacked under the $\wedge$ shaped roof for winter feed.

One morning Charley Thurman came down the path and into the yard. Pa was standing on the porch watching the sun come over the mountains east of the house. It got light long before we could see the sun, as there was a mountain ridge to the east (and most other directions for that matter). Charley sat on the porch and visited a while before he brought up the subject he had come for. "Bill," he said, "you s'pose you could loan us a few dollars to buy some grub?"

Pa knew Charley was willing to work and he was handy with tools, but there was just no work to be had thereabouts at that season of the year. "Come in the house," Pa said. In the living room Don sat in his rocking chair. He could use his hands pretty well yet but had almost given up trying to walk. Pa asked Charley if he thought he could made a wheelchair out of Don's rocker.

Charley studied the chair a while, then said, "I could if I had the stuff to do it with. It'd take some irons and wheels, and I'd have to have a forge and coal an' stuff." The men went back out to the porch to talk over the details. It was decided they would go to Medford the next day and get the material.

"Well, Charley," Pa said, "I'll give you ten dollars for doing the job. Here's five now and you'll get the rest when the wheelchair is finished." They left early the next morning. Usually it took two days for a trip to Medford and back.

The blackberries were getting ripe, and Ma and us kids picked and canned berries. There was a yellow jackets' nest at the edge of the berry patch. They make their nest in a hole in the ground. They hollow out a cavity the size of a teacup, and leave just an entryway the size of a nickel to get in and out. They are sassy things and seem to fly with their stinger forward, 'cause when they hit, the first thing you feel is the sting.

Usually it was Ralph, Glen, Beck (Bessie), and I who picked the berries. Sometimes Glen would get tired of berry picking and he would heave a rock over at the nest. The yellow jackets would come boiling out of their nests "madder 'n hornets." The berry picking would be over for the day. Finally, Ma got tired of that monkey business and told us we had to finish the berries regardless. The yellow jackets were pretty touchy by then, and it didn't take much to rile them up. After dark that evening, Ralph and Glen took Ma's sieve and sneaked up and put it upside down over the opening to the yellow jackets' nest. The next forenoon we finished picking the berries.

After dinner Ma and Beck got busy with the berries, and presently Ma called, "Any you boys seen my sieve?"

"Yeah," Ralph answered, "we put it over the yellow jackets' nest so we could finish picking berries."

"Well, you just go right up and get it," Ma said. "I've got to have it to work these berries."

We went up to the berry patch and found the sieve full of angry wasps. They completely filled the sieve and were fightin' mad. Well, we stood around trying to figure out how to get

These are yellow with black bands. They don't have the thin waist like other wasps, but are more the shape of a bee.

the sieve without getting stung! Glen told Ralph he should get it 'cause he was the biggest. Ralph said no, Glen should get it 'cause he was smaller and not so much room for them to light on him! "Well then, Lynn should get it. He's smaller yet," Glen said.

Well, there wasn't anybody there smaller than me to pass the buck to, so I figured I was elected. I walked over and looked down at the sieve full of angry wasps. The shivers ran up and down my back. They seemed to be buzzing louder all the time. Glen came over and pulled me back a ways. "Now, here's what you do," he said. "You sneak up there and grab the sieve and dive into them thick alder bushes on the other side. Keep your head down and keep runnin'. The bushes will keep the wasps brushed off."

The scheme might have worked, too, but I missed my first grab and just hit the sieve enough to turn it right side up. I turned back and grabbed the rim and dived into the bushes. I got my head in all right, but the yellow jackets found the seat of my pants. I didn't know I could run so fast. Ralph and Glen had run the other way when I started in to pick up the sieve, and even with their head start I got to the yard gate almost by the time they did.

When Pa and Charley came back from Medford, they made arrangements for Charley to work at the blacksmith shop down at Ruch. Pa brought us kids each a little sack of licorice drops. These were almost pure licorice, and were meant to be used for cough drops. They made a brown-colored saliva that looked like tobacco juice, and us kids went around spitting our make believe tobacco juice at every target we could find. This was a cicada year and the big insects were everywhere. They covered the bushes and trees, in places almost end to end. Many a cicada got a licorice juice bath. Glen, however, wasn't satisfied with blasting the cicadas. He'd spit licorice juice on my bare feet and legs every time he'd get close enough. I'd bawl

Screen →

A sieve, sometimes called a colander, used to sieve seeds and skins out of fruit
and stuff.

Licorice drops, about actual size. Old-timers will remember them as a good
way to ease a sore throat.

and throw what cuss words I could manage at him. Ralph got
tired of that finally, and he caught Glen and wrestled him to
the ground and sat on him while he pulled Glen's shirt open
and spit licorice juice all over his belly.

One morning, on my early-morning trip around behind the
woodshed, I saw a huge animal up in the orchard eating the
apples and pears that were under the trees. I ran back into
the house and bust into Pa's bedroom (none of the family were
up yet). "Pa," I hollered, "there's a big black bear up in the
orchard eatin' apples!"

Pa got into his pants and followed me out to the yard gate.
He stood looking at the big animal for some time. "It ain't a
bear," he said, "but I'll be damned if I know what it is." He
went back into the house and got the .30-30. It was getting
lighter now, and Pa stood by the gate and watched while the
big animal worked its way closer to the house. Finally it got
full of apples and started walking toward us at a steady pace.
"I'll betcha a dollar that's Belle, our old sow. Sam McKee said
we would see her sooner or later."

There was a hog trough back of the storehouse. She came
and smelled along the bottom of it for a while, then started
back toward the orchard. Old Lad pushed the yard gate open
and trotted out to where she was. Belle turned facing him and
waited. Laddie trotted up and stuck his nose against her nose

for a moment, then he sniffed all around her and walked over
to an apple tree and left his scent, kicked up a few tufts of sod,
said woof-woof, and came trotting back to the yard.

Belle was no ordinary hog. Weighing a good four hundred
pounds, she didn't appear to have a pound of fat on her. The
arch of her back was as high as the average man's belt buckle.
She was scratched and scarred all over, and her tail had been
bitten off an inch from her body. A tuft of hair like a feather
duster grew from the stump. Her ears were chewed off to rag-
ged stumps, and the slash of a powerful paw had removed one
eye and deep claw marks lined the side of her head and shoulder. She had long tushes on her lower jaw, which no doubt had
ripped open the belly of many an adversary.

Ma then started dumping the dishwater and garbage from
the kitchen into the hog trough, and each day Belle would
come and clean it out. After several days of this, she brought
her five pigs out of the woods into the orchard, where they
helped her clean up the fruit that fell from the trees. The pigs

Belle of the Siskiyous

were tall and long-legged like their mother. They kept to the far side of the orchard and could disappear into the woods quick as a wink, at one warning woof from their mother.

One morning Pa said, "I'm sure buildin' up an appetite for some ham and bacon off from one of them shoats." He took Old Lad through the yard gate and pointed out the pigs to him. "Go catch 'im, Lad," Pa said, giving Lad a push. Laddie took a couple of steps and turned, looking up at Pa. He wagged his tail a little while, then trotted back into the yard. "Hmm," Pa said, "well, I don't blame you."

"Bring the .30–30 out here," Pa said to me, "we're gonna have some spare ribs." Resting the rifle over the gate post, he braced his feet to steady himself, and when the nearest of the young hogs turned broadside to him Pa squeezed the trigger. At the crack of the rifle, the shoat sprang into the air, flipped over backwards, and lay kicking on the ground. The rest of the herd simply vanished into the woods. "Glen, Ralph," Pa called, "go up and drag that shoat down here." As the boys went out of the gate Pa cautioned, "Unless that shoat is plum dead, don't you touch it. One squeal out of it, and old Belle would be on top of you."

The folks went over to Medford about once a month, and many times they would take a wagonload of wood. Everybody burned wood there, and anyone having stove wood or fire-place wood could take the load to the wood yard anytime and get cash for it. Sometimes Pa would take a load to the Iamses, as he and Ma usually stayed overnight with them when they went to Medford. When Pa and Ma were gone from home, Ralph was in command, and any of us who didn't mind had to answer to Pa when they got home, so we were pretty well regulated. At first Perry and Annie Morgan thought that, being the folks were gone, they could just stay at our place all the time. Ralph soon straightened them out on that. After a couple of hours he would just tell them to go home, and they went.

On this trip, the folks brought us all some new clothes. School would soon start, and any of us who wanted to go to school could wear at least some of our new clothes to school. Well, Ralph was growing up and had been to school enough so he could read and write and work any arithmetic he ever expected to need, and Glen said he had gone to school four years and "if I ain't learnt anything in that time, there's no use me goin' any more." So it turned out Beck and I were the first to get to wear our new clothes.

We were getting some cloudy weather and the fall rains were due to set in anytime. We had the storehouse well stocked with dry stove and fireplace wood, also with baskets of apples and pears and boxes of cats and kittens. It didn't seem to matter how many cats we had, we always had plenty of mice.

One cold, drizzly night we were all gathered around the fireplace watching the flames play over the logs in the grate. Ma had filled one of the big iron kettles half full of beans and ham hocks and covered them with water. She hung the kettle on one of the cranes and swung it in over the blazing logs. Soon the aroma of cooking beans and ham filled the room. Conversation had dwindled to nothing, as we were content to watch the embers flare up at times and then die away. Contentment settled over the room.

Then the most ungodly scream filled the room. Most of us sat frozen to our seats. Old Lad bounced to his feet. His hackles standing high on his back, he walked to the door, growling deep in his throat. Then it came again, louder and more piercing than before. If you have ever heard a cat when somebody rocked on his tail with a rocking chair, just amplify that about a thousand times and it will give you an idea of the scream we heard. Ralph threw another log on the fire and the blaze lighted up the room. We all sat looking wide-eyed at each other. "Panther," Pa said. "Maybe two of 'em, probably fightin' over them hog entrails you boys carried out in the brush." Beck got up and lit the lamp. The lighted room helped to calm our pounding hearts.

The next afternoon Miry Thurman came down the trail and into the yard. She wanted, she said, to "borry" our crosscut. The cold rain was coming through the pine boughs, and the dark clouds seemed to sit right on top of the trees. "Better come in and set for a spell," Ma invited. "Get warmed up before you start home."

Miry pulled a chair up before the fireplace. "We're just out of wood," she said, "an' I reckon Perry and me will have to git busy."

"Miry," Ma said, "we heard the greatest scream last night anybody ever heard. It sounded like a woman bein' killed."

"That was a catamount," Miry answered. "There's a lot of them around here. Did I ever tell you about the time one of them varmints chased me home from Alder Spring?" Miry paused, gazing reflectively into the flames in the fireplace. Pa got his plug of tobacco from his pocket and bit off a chew. He handed the plug to Miry, who did likewise. She handed the tobacco back to Pa, and after chewing a spell, she began.

"I was jist a slip of a girl then, 'bout fo'teen I reckon. That was afore old McKee got aholt of this place. We used to live here then. My pap's rumatix got to actin' up and Mom sez, 'Miry, you take the dishpan an' the draw knife an' go up to Alder Spring an' git a pan of hazel bark, to make tea fer your pap.'

"My maw could make the best hazel bark brew in this country. She'd bile down a dishpan of hazel bark, an' she'd git about a half gallon or so of juice. Then, while it was still warm, she'd mix in about the same of good ol' mountain dew. She never let anybody know her 'receit,' 'scept me. A couple a swigs of that, and Pappy was ready to go out an' drag in a bear by the tail. Folks around here called Maw the witch of the Siskiyous."

Miry chewed thoughtfully a little while, then continued. "Well, I wuz down on my knees strippin' bark from them hazel nut bushes when I looked up in a big oak tree there, an' I seen this great big catamount. He was a switchin' his big, long tail back 'n forth an' adiggin' in his claws, gettin' ready to jump. I throwed the draw knife (I shudda kep' it to hack him with), an' I started runnin'. I could hear that big ol' cat comin' down the trail after me. He was so clost I could feel his hot breath on the back of my neck."

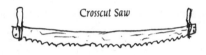

Crosscut Saw

Draw Knife

Miry looked at the circle of wide-eyed listeners. She wiped her hand across the back of her neck and glanced back over her shoulder as if she expected to see her catamount right behind her. She spit a stream of tobacco juice into the fireplace and watched it fry a few moments before she continued.

"There was a six-foot picket fence around this yard then, an', as I could hear that catamount's foot pads ahittin' the trail behind me, I knowed I wouldn't have time to open no gate, so I jumped. I left the ground sixteen feet on t'other side the fence, and landed smack aginst the kitchen door. The big cat slammed aginst the picket fence and I jumped through the door and slammed it shut. That ol' catamount flew into sech a rage, he ripped all the pickets offa the east side of the yard fence."

The first day of school Beck and I donned our new duds, took our dinner buckets, and started out, but before we got out the big gate we began thinking about how dark and dreary the big woods looked along the trail. "Do you s'pose them catamounts are still out there in the woods?" I asked Beck.

"I've been thinkin' about that," she answered, "an' the more I think about it, the less I like it." We went back to the house and asked Ralph if he would walk to school with us.

"You ain't afraid, are you?" Glen asked. "Shucks, I prowl them woods all the time."

"All right," Pa said, "Glen, you walk to school with the kids."

About halfway down the trail there was a giant pine tree. It had been checked for a "shake"* tree many years ago but was never cut down. Big gobs of pitch had run out of the opening and had been burned off.† Many years of this had burned a big hollow back into the tree. The opening was big enough for Beck and me to get back into. We had been to the tree many times through the summer. It was raining by the time we got to the big tree, and Glen suggested Beck and I get back into the hollow until we warmed up a bit. "There's not room for all three of us," he said. "I'll be outside." After a while we decided to go on, and when we came out there was no Glen to be found.

"Do you s'pose a panther got 'im?" I asked, wide-eyed.

"I'm about ready to hope so," Beck answered. "Come on, let's go." We ran the rest of the way to the store, which was in a clearing and not far from the schoolhouse.

Our teacher's name was Grace Darling. Her parents could not have named her better. Of medium height, she was about

---

*To check for a shake tree, two notches are chopped into the trunk, one above the other the length of a shake apart, then the piece is split out. If it splits straight and clean, it is considered a good shake tree.

†During the rainy season people set fires anywhere in the woods. Everything was soaked for about four months in the winter.

seventeen, with soft brown eyes and shining, wavy auburn hair caught together in back with a narrow ribbon tied in a bow. She had a rather slow way of smiling, but when she did smile at us kids, we felt well rewarded.

There were from a dozen to sixteen pupils who ranged from first graders to a couple of big boys who decided (after seeing the teacher) that maybe they could still learn something at school. Teacher boarded with the Kaufmans, whose farm was about a mile down the valley from the schoolhouse.

Vance Buckley also decided to come back to school. Pa bought our cow from the Buckleys, and I met Vance, who was about nineteen, at that time. Orrin Kaufman was about Vance's age, and the two young men were neighbors and good friends. By the end of the first month of school we were well into our studies. Our beloved teacher managed that tough bunch of hillbillies with a gentleness that made us all want to do our best.

The two big boys seemed to require a lot of help from the teacher, it appeared to us littler kids. However, she never played favorites, and we all thought the world of her. We liked the big boys, too. They were good to us kids. They played games with us and sometimes, at teacher's suggestion, they would help with our lessons.

Our main game at recess and noon was baseball. We laid out our diamond in the little clearing. For a ball we had a fairly round rock about the size of a baseball, and for a bat we used a hewed-down pine knot.* We had no gloves or mitts, but we soon learned how to let the ball (rock) hit the ground at least once before we caught it. Once in a while the big boys would catch it on the fly.

---

*These pine knots were from huge logs which had rotted away after many many years. The knots would be two to four feet long and sometimes four or five inches through at the big end. They were very hard, and so full of pitch they wouldn't rot in a thousand years.

We had only seven months of school, but we did not waste any time and we made good progress with our studies. There is no way that two healthy young men can sit and watch such a beautiful girl as our teacher without feeling the pangs of manhood stirring in their hearts. Us kids were worried for fear Orrin and Vance would become jealous of one another and break up their long friendship.

Beck and I took our lessons home and "taught" them to Don. Charley Thurman had finished the wheelchair and now Don could move about the house as he pleased. He was an apt pupil and our "teaching" helped us as well as him. Sometimes we walked to or from school with Perry and Annie, but they were not very regular in their attendance, so we never waited for them. We were no longer afraid we would meet a panther on the trail, as Pa explained panthers were more afraid of us than we were of them.

Some mornings the sun would be bright in our high valley but by the time we got down to the schoolhouse we would be under cloud cover with drizzle and fog. The clouds and fog

Sail to the old village schoolhouse
Anchor outside the school door
Ruch Ore.
1908

with the sun shining on it from above looked like an immense layer of cotton candy all down through the valley and up into the canyons. Sometimes there would be a week of steady drizzle with now and then a shower thrown in. Our little Alder Creek was a brawling little river as it made its way down the steep, rocky creek bed to the river. The Applegate River, which was a couple of miles from our home, was awakening from its summer sleep and was moaning in its rocky bed. Us boys built a shelter out of poles and pine boughs to eat our dinner (as we called lunch) in, so we wouldn't have to eat in the schoolhouse with the girls.

Possumtrot Swamp was now a small lake with wood ducks and muskrats, also a lot of other water dwellers. It was over on the southwest corner of our land, with heavy timber between there and our house. I had been there only a couple of times. In the summer it was a sea of mud. The timber around the swamp was dark and damp, with long sheets of Spanish moss hanging from the limbs. Some of the boys at school told me the place was haunted. There were columbines growing up the shady draws, and on some of the slopes there were acres and acres of manzanita brush, flattened to the ground where the bears had broken it down to feed on the berries. There was no road to the swamp, just some game trails that the natives called possumtrots. Some of these trails found their way over to the deer lick* that was up in the timber behind the reservoir (see map, p. 102).

One time when Glen and I were there we found a large lizard. He was mottled brown and green. He was about eighteen inches long, half of him being tail. Glen hit him with a stick and his tail flew off up close to his body. The lizard

---

*The deer lick was a small hole in the ground filled with salt, placed where natural game trails crossed. Animals came there for salt. A hole big enough for a couple of men was dug about thirty yards away and covered with poles and brush. This was called a blind.

crawled into the slime, but the tail kept flipping and hopping around on the ground. "Perry told me," Glen said, "if the lizard don't find his tail and put it back on before sundown he will die." We caught the tail and put it over behind a deadfall.

Ol' Lad never liked Charley Thurman, so when a knock sounded at the door and Laddie raised his head and growled a sort of disgusted growl we knew it was the Thurmans, there for an evening visit. Sometimes they came for supper, never waiting for an invitation.

Tonight Ma had refilled the big iron kettles, one with beans and the other with diced winter pears. It took about the same length of time to cook both. The cranes were swung in over the coals, and we invited the Thurmans to join us around the fireplace. Outside was the usual drizzle and fog, and sometimes the fireplace would catch a down draft and belch a puff of smoke out into the room. Perry and Annie, Beck and Glen and Don were around the kitchen table playing cards. After the conversation around the fireplace tapered off, I went around and stood by Miry's chair. She put her hand on my shoulder and said, "Hower you tonite, kiddo?"

"I wanted to ask you something," I said. "Some of the boys at school told me Possumtrot Swamp was haunted. Is that the truth?"

"There's hants there, all right," Miry said. She paused and looked over toward Pa. Pa got out his plug of horseshoe and bit off a corner, then handed it to Miry. After she got her chew going good she continued. "One day me an' Charley cut across over to Mike Riser's (pronounced Reezer) to help him bile off a batch of mash. We was there most of the day helpin' with the still an' when we started home there was a light fog acrawlin' up the canyons. It was a purty nite with the moon siftin' its light down through the fog. We come down out of the timber an' there was the swamp spread out afore us.

"Maybe you ain't agoin' to b'lieve this, but there was all

ROAD TO STORE

TO APPLEGATE RIVER

ALDER CREEK

SLOPE COVERED WITH MENZANITA BUSHES

STAND[I]

STUMPS

10 OR 12 ACRES OF PLOW LAND

MOSTLY BRUSH

BIG OAK TREES & UNDER BRUSH

NAT. FOREST

STANDING TIMBER

RAIL FENCE

THICK STANDIN[G]

POSSUM TROT SWAMP

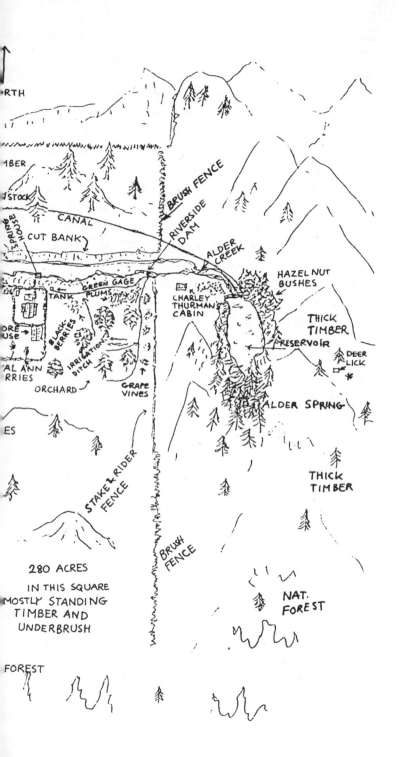

them Chinymun out there aflittin' around over that mud n' water atendin' their cook fires. Mike Riser had told Charley and me that sometimes he would uncork a new jug and go over there and watch them cook their rice."

"How did the Chinamen get there?" I asked, "and what kept them from sinkin' in the mud?"

"They had already sunk in the mud; that was jist their speer-its we seen out there. Them Chinymun used to pan gold along these creeks and along the Applegate. There warn't much gold to be found, but they would keep at it and finally save up a little gold dust. There was some wild mountain people livin' over in them deep woods, an' about the time a Chinyman would git some gold saved up, some o' them mountain people ud sneak up and bop 'im over the head and take his gold. Then they'd tote 'im over to Possumtrot an' tie rocks on 'im and sink him in the mud. There's a bottomless hole out in there aways and them bodies would sink in there an' never come up."

After the Thurmans had gone home I went over to Pa's chair and said, "Pa, do you think Miry really saw those lights and those spirits she told about?"

Pa rubbed his chin reflectively. "Possibly," he said. "There's lights around some swamps called foxfire. It's caused by rotting vegetation givin' off a gas that makes a light under certain con-ditions. The warm air rising from the swamp would cause the fog to crawl and flit around over the swamp. A few swigs from one of Mike Riser's jugs and it would be easy to see pigtails on them fog spirits."

It was getting close to Christmas vacation and we were sum-ming up our first half term of progress. Most of the pupils had made good gains and we were looking forward to coming back to school after Christmas. One day we had a little picnic and played games after we ate our lunch. Our beloved teacher came out and played with us, and that always made us kids

happy. Vance Buckley was still sitting on the log over by our
shelter where us boys ate our lunch. I liked Vance a lot and
wondered why he didn't come and play. After a while I went
over and sat on the log beside him. He was looking down at
the ground, his chin resting in his hand. "Vance," I asked, "are
you sick?"

He sensed the concern in my voice and raised up his head
and looked at me for a little bit. "Yes, in a way you might say
I am." He put his arm around my shoulders. "I'm not coming
back to school after Christmas," he said. At the question in my
eyes, he said, "You will understand sometime, little pal, after
you get to be a man."

We had only one week of Christmas vacation, and during
that week Grace Darling and Orrin Kaufman went over to Jacksonville, which was the county seat, and got married. The news
got back to us before school started the next Monday. We
missed the big boys, and when some of the kids asked the
teacher if "Orrie" wasn't coming back to school, she said, "No,
Orrin isn't coming back. He said to tell you children that he'd
learned his lesson, and now he has to stay at home and work."
She smiled her slow smile, and we knew all was well with the
Kaufmans.

Glen and Ralph had been spending some nights in the blind
at the deer lick. They loaded some shells with buckshot for an
old double-barreled shotgun that had been left in the house.
This old gun had side hammers and was rusty in spots, but it
seemed to shoot all right. The boys would take turns watching
the lick and sleeping. The nights when the moon was full, even
if it was cloudy, they could see plain enough to outline an
animal if it came to lick salt. That was the reason for the shotgun and buckshot.

One morning they came down the trail carrying a deer. It
was a young doe, about full grown and in good flesh. They had

gutted her out up at the lick, and tied her feet together and hung her on a pole, which they carried on their shoulders. They were pretty proud. Ralph told the story like this. "It was my turn to stay awake. I had been sleepin' since midnight, an' it was about three o'clock, so I took my seat by the peephole. Glen soon went to sleep an' I settled down to watch. I was still kinda sleepy, and I musta dozed, 'cause all at once there was this deer there lickin' salt. I began to get shaky, so I thought I better shoot while I could. I don't know whether I pulled both triggers, or whether the jolt from the first shot jarred the other hammer loose. Anyway, when the smoke cleared away the deer was layin' there on the ground, an' I had two empty shells in the gun."

"Didn't it kick awful hard?" I asked Ralph.

"I don't remember that it kicked at all," Ralph answered. "We was so excited about gettin' the deer, we come off and left the shotgun up there!"

Pa had been having some wheezing spells, and as the weeks wore on toward Easter without hardly a break in the rainy weather, he began to wonder if Oregon was the best place for a man with the asthma after all. Beck and I were in school, but the rest of the family had a hard time finding something interesting to do. Don still had the use of his hands, and with some help from Glen and Ralph, he made a violin from a cigar box. He and Ralph would play duets, with Ralph on the harmonica and Don on his cigar box fiddle. Old Lad could stand that about so long, and then he would join in with that big tenor voice of his. One day Don said, "Make that damn dog go outdoors. Its bad enough, havin' to keep in tune with Ralph, without Ol' Lad drownin' us both out." Don had a lot of talent and plenty of time to study, and he kept up with, or maybe a little ahead of, Beck and I in our lessons. He was good in mental arithmetic, and sometimes would help us with our homework. He also liked to play cards and was a real sharp player.

Belle, our old sow, came back to the farmstead a few times during the winter, and us kids would sort out some of the poorer apples and pears and throw them over the picket fence to her. We never did see any of her pigs again.

At Easter time, the Iamses sent word that we should come spend Easter with them. We talked it over and decided that Pa and Ma should go, and the rest of us stay at home and look after the stock and chickens. During Christmas vacation Pa and Ralph had gone down the valley and bought several sacks of oats and barley. These they stacked up in the barn out of the rain. Our brown Leghorn hens were laying an egg or two now and then, and Silk, our cow, was giving us a couple of gallons of milk a day. We had venison, beans, stewed pears, and sourdough bread, and plenty of dry wood in the storehouse. We never did have all the eggs we wanted, so we decided we would all hunt eggs while the folks were gone and on Easter day each of us could eat the eggs he had found. Because Don couldn't get out and hunt eggs, we agreed to share with him.

I had a Union Leader tobacco sack that I was carrying my eggs in as I hunted. The old Union Leader sacks had a flap to fold down over the opening, with a strong cord to wrap around so it could be carried in the pocket. I had two eggs in the sack and was carrying it by the cord when Glen came to me and said, "Whatcha carryin' them rocks around for?" He hit the sack with a broken fence picket he had in his hand. I set up a howl, and he said, "Gee whiz, I thought sure them was rocks." I went into the house and emptied the eggs out of the sack into a pan and tried to sort the broken shells from the egg, but it was no use. On Easter day we decided to put all the eggs together and take them down to the store and trade them for cheese and crackers.

Glen was full of mischief and was always playing tricks on the rest of us, but we had lots of fun together. The day after Easter the folks were not expected home, so Glen said to me,

"Get the Piper* and let's go squirrel huntin'."

"I ain't got any shells," I answered.

He had the shotgun in his hand and he dug around in his pockets and found three .22 shorts. "Here," he said, "if you get a squirrel with each of them, that will be enough." We took Ol' Lad (or he took us) and went out into the big timber. The deep woods were damp and in some places quite dark. It was way past noon before Laddie treed a squirrel. It was in a big tree, and it took us a long time to locate it. "You go around the tree," Glen said. "If you see him, shoot. If he comes around on my side, I'll shoot."

I located the squirrel, all right, and I took careful aim and thought I heard the bullet go plunk. Those big grays are hard to knock out of a tree. "He's comin' around to my side," Glen said. Then the 12-gauge went boom and the squirrel came tumbling down through the branches. Glen picked it up. "I'm so hungry," he said, "I could eat him hide, hair and all."

"I'll eat the other half," I said. "Why don't we make a fire and roast him?"

We skinned and gutted the squirrel, and Glen dug around in his pockets for matches. "You got any matches?" he asked. He finally found one match. About half of it was broken off. "Here," he said, "you make a fire while I find the sticks to string him on!"

"You expect me to make a fire with that little stub of a match?" I asked.

"Lynn," he said, "you make a fire with that or I'll make you walk back home after another match." These matches were sulphur block matches. They were made by splitting a block of wood into tiny squares, the bottom of the block having been bruised so it would hold together. Then the tips were

*The Piper was a little single-shot .22 rifle.

covered with some kind of sulphur mixture and let dry. It was the only kind of matches we had there.

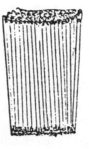

Sulphur Matches

Well, I dug back under an old rotted log that the bears had torn apart looking for grubs and wood ants until I finally found some dry pine needles and some punky wood that was fairly dry. I built a tiny little tepee out of the needles and slivered the punky wood and laid it up against the sides. I left a little door in the front of the tepee to stick the lighted match in (if it lit). When you strike these matches, at first there is a little blue green glow at the tip. Then, while you hold your breath for what seems ever so long, the glow starts to turn red, then blazes up into a tiny flame. I found a dry chip, and with it in my left hand I laid down on my belly facing my little pine needle tepee. I held my breath and scratched the little match on the chip. A faint glow appeared and seemed too small ever to make a flame. Finally it blazed up and I held it under the pine needles.

When I got the fire going good, Glen pushed two forked sticks into the ground, one on either side of the fire, and laid the green stick with the squirrel strung it on across them. We left it over the fire until we could pull it apart. The outside got pretty hard and black. "I wish we had some salt," I said, as I chewed on a ham. After we finished the squirrel we started

back home. It seemed a lot farther back than it did coming out.

Uncle Jim Scott and Aunt Matt came to visit us that spring.
They stayed a couple of weeks. One day while they were there,
Uncle Jim said to us boys, "Let's build a little log cabin in the
fireplace, and then burn it down so we can see what a log cabin
looks like when it's afire." They went into the storehouse and
got a lot of pine firewood that had been split up for the cook
stove. They smoothed off a place in the big fireplace and built
the cabin. The weather had been cloudy and rainy most of the
time since they came, and Uncle Jim complained about being
cold. As the flames licked up through the pine sticks in the
little cabin, Uncle Jim rubbed his hands together and said,
"Now I'm finally gonna get warm."

In a short time, the flames filled the fireplace and licked out
around the edges. The heat from the furiously burning pitch
pine was so intense it drove us to the other side of the room.
The mantle shelf started to blaze and Pa yelled at the boys,
"Grab some buckets and carry water from the tank. Hurry up!"
We all got busy carrying water in buckets, kettles, dishpans, or
anything we could get hold of. Ralph and Uncle Jim threw the
water at the mantle above the fireplace. We were a pretty
scared bunch for a while. We thought the house was going to
go. After we got the fire under control, Pa looked over at
Uncle Jim and asked, "Well, did you finally get warm?" Pa was
breathing hard by now. The smoke and excitement had
brought on a spell of asthma, and he had to go out into the
yard and sit by a tree until it eased up.

Uncle Jim enjoyed the mountains and the big timber. He
was interested in everything around, and many times he and I
would ramble around over the place. I showed him a hornets'
nest high up in a laurel tree, and he said, "I'd sure like to have
one of those things to take back home for a souvenir."

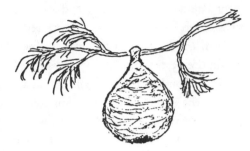

Bald-faced Hornet
about actual size

These nests are sometimes as
big as a gallon jug. They are made
of a gray-colored stuff like
chewed-up paper.

"Them's bald-faced hornets," I said. "Don't ever go near one of their nests. They could kill a person."

"You ever get stung by one of them?"

"Yes, I did," I answered. "One time one came in the house and I was tryin' to shoo him out. All at once he came straight at me and hit me on the temple. It felt like I'd been hit with a big club. It knocked me flat on the floor."

Sometime later, Pa and Uncle Jim were going to the store with the team and wagon. Uncle Jim saw a hornets' nest off the road a piece and said, "Bill, let's get that nest. I want it to take home with me."

"You propose to take it hornets and all?"

"Look, I've got a plan," Uncle Jim said. "It's cold and rainy, so they are all inside. They won't be very lively when it's cold and wet like this. You drive under the nest and stop. I can reach it if I stand up in the wagon. I'll twist up my handker-chief and stick it in the hole in the bottom, then I'll cut it loose and we'll take it home and sink it in the tank until the hornets all drown. Then I'll shake them out and I'll have the nest."

Pa drove under the nest and stopped. Uncle Jim climbed

over behind the spring seat and stood up in the wagon. He twisted up his handkerchief and started poking it up into the hole in the bottom of the nest. A loud buzzing came from inside the nest, and in his eagerness to get the hole closed up, Uncle Jim pushed too hard and broke a piece out of the bottom of the nest. The hornets came swarming out.

Pa brought the lines down across the horses' rumps and yelled, "Git!" The team lunged forward and Pa whipped them into a gallop. It was downgrade to the store, and they came out into the clearing as tight as the team could run. The hornets didn't follow them out of the timber, and Pa pulled the team to a stop in front of the store. Uncle Jim picked himself up off the floor of the wagon. "Good God, man," he said to Pa, "you sure gave me a shakin' up."

"You're damn lucky to be alive," Pa answered. "Next time you want to catch a nest full of hornets, don't ask me to help."

As we got further into spring, the warm sunshine broke through the clouds more often and the snow in the higher canyons added its runoff to the many creeks and tiny rivulets. The Applegate River became a roaring tide as it tumbled down its steep and rocky bed. The noise carried up the canyons and draws and filled the foothills with sound. Ralph and Glen plowed and planted the oats in the field, and we all found something to do. Our chickens sometimes went across the creek and up the side of the mountain on the other side. There were insects and sprouting seeds among the layers of damp leaves and grass. There was underbrush and timber with open spaces here and there. These open spots were where the flock usually scratched for food. Coyotes and chicken hawks preyed on them, and the roosters would post themselves around the outer edge of the flock to keep watch. One day we heard a loud squawking and commotion from up there, and the whole flock took wing and flew clear across the canyon, circled the trees by the fence, and lit in the backyard. They looked for the world like a flock of pheasants and appeared to fly about as well.

Although summer was always hot and dry, we looked forward to it after the long, cold, drizzly winter. Some of the hens stole their nests out, and with the few that Ma "set" in the chicken coop, we started the summer with two or three dozen young chicks. There were a number of chicken hawks there that preyed on the young chickens. They were sly, and very fast flyers; we called them swifts. They would light in a tree and watch their chance, then dive down and pick up a chick and fly away. One day I saw one of them light in the very tip of the big pine down by our west gate. I went and told Pa. After looking at it a bit, Pa said, "Go get me the .30–30." I brought him the gun and he sat down on the porch floor. He folded his handkerchief and laid it on the porch railing. He rested the gun across it and took careful aim. At the crack of the gun the hawk spread its wings, then toppled out of the tree, dead. "That's one less of the blasted things," he said.

As we moved into summer our troubles seemed to multiply. Ralph came in one morning and asked, "Who left the big gate open?" We all looked at one another.

"Nobody's been out there. Why?" Pa asked.

"Dick and Maud and Silk are all out and gone," Ralph said. "Their tracks go out the gate."

Pa called Glen. "Go along with Ralph," he said, "and follow those tracks. The sooner you start, the easier it will be to follow."

The boys took halters and a feed bucket half full of oats. The tracks followed the road for a distance, then the cow tracks left the road and went up a grassy draw. "You follow the cow," Ralph said; "I'll follow the horses." At the turnoff to the oat field, the tracks left the main road and followed the trail to the field. The oats were up, with a fresh green cover over the ground. Maud and Dick were out in the field grazing on the fresh green crop. The rails had been laid down on the ground, making an opening in the fence. Ralph walked out to the team shaking the oats around in the bucket. He put the halters on them and led them out of the field. Then, after tying them to a bush, he laid the rails back up, closing the gap in the fence. He soon caught up with Glen, who was leading Silk up the road towards home.

A few days later, Pa announced plans to go on a fishing trip. We loaded the tent and some bedding and food, also some oats for the team, and a fifty-gallon vinegar barrel into the wagon. Pa never was much of a hand to talk over his plans ahead of time. "What in the world are you gonna do with that barrel?" Ma asked.

"That's to put the fish in," Pa answered. "We are gonna leave early in the morning, so here is the way we will do it. Glen and Becky both got a trip to Medford with us, so now Ralph and Lynn will go along. This time, I'm goin' to put Don in charge here while we are gone. Remember now, what he says goes while we are gone. He will report to me when we get back."

It was a big day's drive from McKee's Mill to Gold Ray Dam. There was a state fish hatchery there, and in the spring when the salmon made their spawning run up the rivers, man sought to improve on nature by catching the salmon and removing the eggs and hatching them in specially prepared ponds, after which they planted the small "fry" upstream in the same waters the fish were headed for in the first place. After the eggs were taken from the salmon the fish were killed* and given to anyone who wanted them.

We arrived at the dam a little before sundown and set up our tent and made camp. The fishery personnel were just fin-

---

*Salmon make only one spawning run in a lifetime, so the practice was not as wasteful as it would first seem.

ishing their day's work and had a number of fish in the boat ready to take to shore. We were camped just a little ways from the water's edge, and they beached their boat by our camp.

Pa and Ralph went down to the boat and talked to the men a while, then they came back carrying some fish. Ralph was carrying one almost as long as he was. "The men in the boat said this one weighed over thirty pounds," he told Ma, "but they said not to fry it. They have some little ones for us to cook for supper." After supper we dressed the fish and cut them into slabs and packed them in the barrel and covered them with salt.

The next day there wasn't much for us to do until the fishermen made their haul. The dam was not very high, and was made especially for the hatchery's use. However, the salmon couldn't jump over it to get upstream. There was a large fish wheel across the dam from where we were camped. This wheel was powered by water from the spillway and was used to regulate the number of fish in the stilling basin below the dam. When the wheel was turning, it picked up fish from below and deposited them above the dam. That way, there were some fish making their normal run upstream. The basin below the dam was jammed with fish that had come upstream and were stopped below the dam. The water was clear and not very deep, and the salmon lay in there like cordwood.

About two o'clock, two boats put out from the fish corral. There were three men in each boat, two oarsmen and one net handler. They went to the lower end of the basin and strung the net across between the boats. By the time they got back to the corral (sorting pen), we could see why they needed two oarsmen to each boat.

The sorting pen was made of planks, and was about twenty or thirty feet square. The sides were about five feet high. It had a plank floor and held about two feet of water. The men tied the boats, one on each side of the gate, then they got out of the boats and pulled the net into the sorting pen by hand. The hardest part was yet to come, however. This turned out to be a real rodeo.

They would catch a fish and check to see if the spawn was ripe. If not, they would toss the fish back into the water below the dam. If the eggs were ready, they would "milk" them into buckets, to be taken to the hatching ponds. After the eggs were taken, they would kill the fish and drop it into one of the boats. Sometimes it would take three men to subdue one of those large salmon. With all the splashing of water and the thrashing around in the sorting pen, it was easy to see those men earned their pay.

By the end of the third day we had the fifty-gallon barrel half full of slabs of salmon, each layer covered with salt as they were built up. After that first evening we always picked out the smaller fish, as they were lots better flavored and finer meat than the big ones. We started home the next morning, and by the time the sun got well up over the ridge we were already to Grants Pass. The road from there to Medford was good and Pa let the horses (or rather, horse and mule) trot part of the time. We stopped and had dinner with the Iamses and left them some fish. Ma took a couple of slabs and went down to the place where we had camped, and visited with the lady there a while after dinner.

When we got home that evening, Glen, Don, and Beck were all full of questions about our trip. "The first fish I brought out," Ralph said, "was almost as tall as I was, and the man said it would weigh about thirty pounds. We ate so many fish I don't think I'll want any for a while."

Pa then asked Don, "How'd everything go?"

Don was pleased at the importance of the part he had in running the place while we were gone. "Oh, pretty good, I guess. Charley came down a couple of times and wanted Glen to come help him stake out a new fence line through the orchard. I told Glen not to go, and Charley got mad and said I had no business tellin' my older brother what to do."

The next couple of days we spent fixing up a smokehouse and getting the salt brushed off the fish and getting the fish started to smoke cure. Next day Charley came down the trail early. Pa was out in the yard and Charley stopped there to talk. "Bill," he said, "we just as well get that fence moved down on the line where it belongs."

"What's wrong with where it is?" Pa asked.

"It's about a hundred yards over on my land; that's what's wrong. I got a surveyor's compass and sighted it out, an' the fence ain't on the line at all. That strip used to be ours, but when old McKee got aholt of this place, he put the fence clear up where it is now."

"I'll tell you what I'll do," Pa said. "You go over to Jacksonville and get the county surveyor to come out and shoot the line again, an' if it's not where it belongs, we will move it over."

"I don't need no county surveyor. I know how to run a compass. You're just tryin' to steal the best part of my land, that's all."

"Them's not very kind words, Charley!" Pa said. Charley turned and stalked off up the trail towards home.

"Charley didn't stay long," Ma said as Pa came into the house.

"No, Charley's kind of hot-tempered. Remember the time he was helpin' put new boards in the porch floor and he got mad at the saw and threw it clear down into the creek, then had to go get it before he could finish the job? I don't know exactly what's back of this, but it may be more than the line fence."

A few days later Ma was looking out the east window when she said, "Who in the world is that comin' down the trail?" It wasn't anybody any of us had ever seen before. They came up to the open kitchen door and Ma went to the door.

"Howdy," the man said. "I'm Bill Thurman, Charley's brother. This's my family. Our cabin burnt down an' we come down to Charley's but they didn't have much to eat in the house, so they sent us on down here. Could you put us up fer a day or two until we can find somewhere to go to?"

Ma, who was kind-hearted to a fault, said, "I guess so, if you are willing to sleep on the floor."

"'Twon't be nothin' new to us," Bill Thurman said, "an' it'll sure beat sleepin' out on the wet ground."

Ma cooked up a big dinner of beans, salmon, sourdough bread, and applesauce. The rest of the family consisted of Bill's wife, a bedraggled-appearing woman who looked like she had been tired ever since she could remember; a girl possibly in her teens; and a hollow-eyed boy of six or seven. There wasn't much conversation during the meal, as everybody was too busy eating.

After dinner Bill Thurman said to Pa, "If you got any work to do, I'm sure willin' to help."

"We cut wood when there's nothin' else to do," Pa told him. "By the way, what happened to your cabin?"

"Well, the fireplace was built outa sticks an' gumbo mud, an' finally the mud all cracked off an' the sticks got afire. It was in the night. Sure a good thing we slep' with most of our clothes on. All I saved was my rifle."

It wasn't long before Chickie (that's what they called the girl)* had marked Ralph for conquest. By the next day she was following him around and asking all kinds of questions. She wasn't getting anywhere with Ralph. Finally she said, "Ralph, you're so big and strong, I'll bet you could pick me up in your arms and carry me easy."

Ralph answered, "Mebby I could, but I sure as hell wouldn't. Now go away and leave me alone."

*Bill Thurman's wife was descended from early Spanish stock and the name Chiquita had filtered down to Chickie.

That was plain enough, even for Chickie, so she turned her attention to Glen. She had better success with Glen, who had always had an abiding curiosity about girls. She followed Glen around for a while, then Glen started following her around.

Beck told Chickie, "You better leave Glen alone or you'll have your cousin Annie in your hair. She claims him for her own."

"Nuts to cousin Annie," Chickie said. "I ain't afraid of her. I know more about boys than she'll ever know."

The affair hadn't gone unnoticed, however, and Ma followed them the next day into the storehouse, where they had gone at Chickie's invitation to watch the kittens play. They were not exactly watching the kittens. Ma grabbed Glen by the collar and picked up the first thing she got her hand on, which happened to be a broken-off shovel handle. She really walloped him good.

Ralph and Bill Thurman were sawing wood down by the barn and Pa was sitting on the front porch sweating his way through an attack of asthma. Ma came up the porch steps. "Pa," she said, "you've got to get those people away from here, right today. I won't have them here another night." The finality of the statement left no room for argument. Pa put on his hat and went down to the barn where Ralph and Bill Thurman were at work.

"Round up your family," he said to Bill. "I've got a place for you to go to work." To Ralph he said, "Hitch up the team and throw some hay in the wagon for the kids to set on."

Some hours later, Pa stopped the team at the quarry office door. He handed the lines to Bill Thurman and climbed down off the wagon and entered the office. "Well, we are not runnin' at full capacity right now," the foreman said, at Pa's question, "but we may get goin' in a week or so. They can stay in one of the bunkhouses until then I guess."

At the bunkhouse door the woman and kids climbed out

and went into the cabin. Bill Thurman stood by the wagon a bit, then said, "I sure want to thank you fer helpin' out. Mebby I c'n help you out some day."

Pa handed him a five-dollar bill. "Here's your first week's pay," he said. "Your regular job won't start for a week yet. In the meantime, find something worthwhile to do around here and get busy."

"Perry and Charley's been doin' something up in the orchard while you were gone yesterday," Ma told Pa the next morning. "What do you s'pose they're up to?"

"Hard to tell," Pa said. "Ralph, take the grubbin' hoe and go up in the orchard and see what Charley and Perry were doin' up there yesterday. You might grub some of them green gage plum sprouts out from around the grape vines while you're up there."

After dinner Ralph picked up the shotgun and said, "Think I'll mosey over and visit with Mike Riser a while." He whistled to Ol' Lad and took off across the clearing toward the thick timber. Pa got the hoe and went around north of the house to the garden and started hoeing out weeds. The soil was rich and we had loads of vegetables. One of the irrigation ditches followed the north edge of the orchard down to the tank by the yard fence, and from there it led over to the garden, so during the hot, dry part of the summer the garden had plenty of moisture.

After a while Pa came back and hung up the hoe and went over and sat on the porch. The sweat was running down his face and he was laboring to get his breath. "Dammit," he said, "I was in hopes this would leave me when the weather got hot and dry." He was still sitting on the porch, leaning back against the rail post, when Ralph came home. Pa slept whenever he could, because sometimes he couldn't sleep when he was in bed and would go out into the open air and sit on the porch.

Ralph came up and stood at the foot of the steps. "Pa," he

said, "I'm worried about Mike Riser. I was over to his place this afternoon and he wasn't home."

"What's wrong with that?" Pa said. "He was probably at the store."

"No, I went down to the store, and Cap said he hadn't seen Mike for several days."

"Where did you get acquainted with Mike?" Pa asked.

"I met him on the trail one time when I was huntin'. We talked a while, and when he found out where I lived and who I was, he said, 'C'mon down to my house and have a cup of coffee.' He fixed some sandwiches and I stayed and visited for 'bout an hour."

"Did you know he was a moonshiner?"

"Not then I didn't. Next time I was there, he told me about it. He said it was the only way he could get any money. I'm sure he's not been home for several days, because his hogs and chickens are out of feed and water. He keeps his dog tied up, an' the poor thing was about starved. I know Mike wouldn't treat his animals that way. I fed and watered everything. His door was open an' the stuff left on the table was dried in the dishes. I looked all around there and hollered; no trace of him."

Next morning Ralph said, "I'm goin' back over to Mike's place and do some more lookin' around. Mike had a bad knee; he mighta fell someplace and broke a leg or something."

Along in the forenoon Charley Thurman came striding down the trail. Pa was sitting on the back porch, and he could see Charley was worked up about something. Charley opened the gate and came up to the porch. "Bill," he exploded, "You gotta do somethin' about that boy of yours!"

"I've got four boys, Charley," Pa said mildly. "Which one should I do somethin' about?"

"About Ralph, that's which one. That kid's apt to kill somebody sometime."

"What's he done now?" Pa asked.

"He went up there and knocked out all them stakes me and Perry set for the new fenceline, an' when I went over an' cussed him out about it, he chased me back over the fence with the grubbin' hoe."

"Sounds like Ralph," Pa said. "He sure don't like to be cussed out."

"Well, we're gonna start movin' that fence tomorra, an' I want you to bring some help an' be there."

"I'll be there!" Pa said. Charley left then and Pa sat for some time thinking over the developments.

When Ralph came home that evening, we were all curious to know what he had found out. "I've been lookin' all day," he said. "Went clear over behind Copple's gulch. Never found a trace of him. Whatcha s'pose could've happened to him?"

"Hard to tell," Pa answered. "Far as I know, he didn't have any relatives around here." After a pause Pa continued, "You better go back over in the morning and turn his livestock loose so they can shift for themselves. Otherwise leave everything as it is."

The next morning after Ralph left, Pa put on his coat and went out the kitchen door. Glen went out on the porch after him. "I'm goin' with you, Pa," he said.

Pa stopped and looked at Glen a little while, then a slow grin spread over his face. "Thanks for the offer," he said, "but this is my show. I'll have to run it my way. You stay here and get the chores done. Ralph probably won't be home till afternoon."

When Pa got up to the fence there was nobody there. Pa rested his stub arm on a post and drew several deep breaths. "Just hope my damn asthma don't flare up," he thought.

He didn't have long to wait. Charley came striding down the trail from his cabin, all the arrogance he could muster showing in his face. He stopped in front of Pa and looked up and down the fence. "Where's the help you was gonna bring?

You don't expect me to move this fence all by myself, do ya?"

"Charley," Pa said in an even voice, "you're not goin' to move any fence, now or ever, an' if you pull one post in this fence, I'll have the sheriff on your back so quick you won't know where he come from."

Charley's face turned purple with rage. He took a few steps back up the trail and picked up a rock the size of a large turnip. He came back and stopped a dozen feet from Pa. "I've got a notion to knock your head right offa yore shoulders," he said.

Keeping his voice even, Pa said, "I'll never let you get close enough to do that."

The purple left Charley's face and his shoulders sagged a bit. "Uh huh!" he said, "you've got that goddam gun on ya, ain'tcha? I wondered why you had yore coat on when it's this warm." Pa kept his unblinking gaze riveted on Charley's face. The arrogance that Charley had brought down the trail had all left him now. He scuffed his feet in the dirt a few times, tossed the rock aside, and without another word turned and went back up the trail toward his cabin. Pa stood by the fence a few minutes to let his breathing get back to normal, then, spying the rock Charley had tossed aside, he climbed over the fence and picked it up.

After Pa left the house that morning, we all had a spell of jitters. "Ma," Beck asked, "what is this all about? Pa looked so sort of grim when he left this morning."

Glen came in from doing the chores. "I'm goin' up to the east fence and see what's goin' on."

"Pa told you to stay here," Ma told him. "Don't you think you better do as he says?"

"He told me to do the chores, an' I've got them done."

Halfway up the trail, Glen met Pa coming down. "Where you headin'?" Pa asked.

"Just goin' up to see if I could help. Whatcha carryin' that rock for?" Pa handed Glen the rock and they came down the trail together. Pa hung his coat on the back of a buckskin-bottomed chair and sat down. Glen, still holding the rock, asked, "What about this rock?"

"That's a souvenir," Pa told him. The rest of us stood there as puzzled as Glen. Pa got out his tobacco and bit off a piece. "That's a rock Charley was gonna knock my head off with," he said.

"How come he didn't?" Glen wanted to know.

"Well, when I told him I'd never let him get close enough, he got suspicious of what I had under my coat and he changed his mind."

"What would you have done if he had't changed his mind?" Glen wanted to know.

Pa chewed a while, then he took aim at a rock a dozen feet out in the yard and splattered it with tobacco juice. "I'd have spit tobacco juice in his eyes," he said.

As we got farther into summer, the hot sun and cloudless days dried the forests, and the dead leaves and pine needles made an ever present threat of fire. We could see smoke over in the Cascade mountains, and news came up the stage road of forest fires burning there. Pa cautioned us often about being careful with fire.

After the hassle with the Thurmans was over, it was a relief not to have them under foot all the time. There was no news about Mike Riser. Ralph had gone back once after the day he turned Mike's livestock loose. Everything was just as he had left it; the hogs and chickens and the dog had gone off into the woods to fend for themselves and there was no sign that anybody had been at the cabin. Ralph was downcast, because he counted Mike as a good friend.

As the days went by, the smoke over in the Cascades became more dense and widespread. We couldn't see the flames in the daytime yet, but at night we would sit out on the west porch and watch the flames run up the trees and balloon out at the top like skyrockets. By the Fourth of July we had the oat hay made and stacked in the ∧ shaped hay barn.

The Thurmans had been along the road to the store several times, and sometimes Charley would go mornings and come back in the evening when there was any work to do at the blacksmith shop. Perry and Annie came up the road one day shooting off firecrackers, and Pa sent Glen down to the road to tell them not to shoot firecrackers along there because the slope on the other side of the road was covered with dried leaves and slashings. This was not a public road, but was the old logging road to McKee's sawmill, and was our property.

A few nights later we heard firecrackers and could see flashes as they exploded. Someone was coming up the road and would stop and shoot a firecracker about every so far. "I'll bet that's Perry," Pa said. "He's showin' us he can shoot firecrackers if he wants to."

"Bring me the .30–30," he said to me. "We will do a little celebrating, too." When Perry got about direct across from the house, he stopped. Pa could make out his outline against the cutbank, and when he lit a match to light his firecracker, Pa aimed four or five feet to one side and fired. The soft-nosed bullet thudded into the cutbank and showered Perry with particles of dried clay and gravel. He let out a yelp and took off up the road as fast as he could run. Pa levered another round into the rifle and fired straight up into the air. "That's just to make him run faster," he said.

Pa's asthma had not improved this summer as it had the first summer, and he was having seizures about as often as he did in the winter. By the time school started and the drizzly weather closed in, he thought he was even worse. One bright morning with the sun shining down upon the fog in the valley, Ma was looking out the east window. "Look who's comin' down the trail," she said. "I do believe it's Charley."

Pa went out and stood on the kitchen porch. Charley came through the gate and stopped a few yards from Pa. "Bill," he said, "I hate to bother you this way, but I wonder if I could get you to haul me and my family over to Quarry Hill?" Then he went on, "There's nobody else around with a team and wagon. My brother Bill sent word that they needed a donkey engineer and if I would come over, I could get the job."

"Sure, Charley," Pa answered, "anything to help a neighbor. Go home and get your stuff gathered up. I'll be there in a little bit with the team and wagon."

We saw them go down the logging road toward the store. Miry was sitting up on the spring seat beside Pa, and Charley and the children were in the wagon box with their belongings. On the stage road they headed toward Quarry Hill, and after discussing the forest fire, which was being slowly pinched out by the increasing fog and drizzly weather, Miry asked, "Bill, did I ever tell you about the time them white grapes up in yore orchard saved Perry's life?"

Pa got out his plug of tobacco and bit off a corner. He handed the plug to Miry, who did likewise. After they had chewed for a while, Pa took aim at a rock beside the road and splattered it with tobacco juice. "No," he said, "how'd it happen?"

Miry took aim at a rock on her side of the road but farther away and splattered *it* with tobacco juice. She turned and winked at Pa. "Well," she said, "I'd been over in the valley pickin' prunes. Don't know how many thousand boxes I musta picked. Anyways, there was little Perry (he was just a tyke then) alayin' in his little bed so sick he couldn't lift his little hand. I knowed right off what was the matter. He had the kollery morbus, so I gethered up some gunny sacks and made a little hammock and put Perry in it. I toted 'im over to that big vine that climbs all over that crooked old oak tree and hung the hammock in among them big five-pound bunches of grapes.

We had our garden down there that year; that was b'fore old McKee got aholt of it, and I worked in the garden all afternoon. When I come back that evenin' little Perry had et all the grapes he could reach an' then climbed out of his little hammock and was a settin' up astraddle of one of them big oak limbs."

Pa didn't get home until almost dark that evening. The clouds had filled our little valley and a cold drizzle filled the air. Ralph heard the wagon coming and went down and opened the big gate. He sent Pa on up to the house while he took care of the team.

"Well, how do you like school?" Ma asked after our first week. "What's your teacher like?"

"Oh, all right, I guess. Teacher's a middle-aged woman (mid-twenties), wears glasses, not very friendly."

"How many kids are comin' this year?"

"Not as many as last, but we've still got a dozen or so."

With the fruit picked and stored, and plenty of wood put away in the dry, there wasn't much to do. As the winter progressed, the rain and fog made the days seem endless. Pa's asthma seizures became more frequent and the general morale dropped to a new low. We missed the Thurmans, although none of us would admit it. Don sawed on his cigar box fiddle and Ralph played mournful tunes on his harmonica, with Old Lad joining in with his big tenor when the music got too heart-rending. We still had plenty of smoked salmon, but we were all so tired of it we shunned it mostly.

The week before Christmas we got sad news. One of the farmers from down the valley stopped at the schoolhouse and talked in low tones to the teacher for a while, then left. Teacher went to the front of the room and turned to face us kids. "Children," she said, "I just got word that our beloved friend, Grace Kaufman, died in childbirth."

After a couple minutes of deep silence, one of the girls asked, "Does that mean she died while havin' her baby?"

"Yes," teacher said, "she died while having her baby."

Bessie slid out of her seat, got her coat and dinner bucket, and left the schoolhouse. Teacher stood silent for a while, then she said, "I'm going to dismiss school for the rest of this week. Christmas vacation starts next week anyway, so you won't have to come back until after Christmas."

When I got home, Ma met me at the door. "What's the matter with your sister?" she asked. "She went into her room and locked the door."

"We got word that Grace Darling died havin' her baby," I answered. "Teacher let school out."

Our holidays that winter were neither merry at Christmas nor happy at New Year's. After a couple more weeks fighting for his breath and cursing the weather, Pa announced he was going south somewhere and try to find a place where the sun shone once in a while. "I'll write," he said as he took the train, "as soon as I find a place where I can get my breath."

The mail came out to Ruch two or three times a week, and we had to go down to the store after it. Beck and I always stopped on the way home from school to see if there was any mail for us. Along in February the long-awaited letter came. Beck and I ran most of the way home with it. Ma opened the letter and read.

> Pomona, California
> February 10, 1910

Dear folks,

I have finally found us a house. I've been staying with my uncle, Spencer Fouty, here in Pomona for the past few weeks. The weather is nice here at the present time.

I traded the farm there for a house and one acre of ground here in Pomona. Pack just our clothes and bedding, everything else stays just as it is. The people I traded with will get to Medford on the 15th. You are to meet them there with the team and wagon. Get your tickets and have everything ready. They will take the team back to their new home, and you board the train for Pomona, Cal. When you get to Pomona, leave the baggage at the depot and walk to 1115 South Hamilton. That is our new home. Don't forget to tell Cap Ruch good-by.

As ever,

Pa

W. H. Scott

P.S. Pack the guns and ammunition box, with the tent, in the big wooden box. Be sure to rope everything good and tight. Thank the Iamses for their help. See you soon.

❰❱

Epilogue

❰❱

The Scott family followed W. H. Scott (Pa) to Pomona, California, in the spring of 1910 and made their home at 1115 South Hamilton Street for the next two years. In a departure from earlier practice in the family life, when they had all lived and worked together in relative isolation from neighbors, they now lived as an urban family. Ralph and Glen, the author's brothers, continued to live at home but held various jobs at brickyards and rose gardens, and picked fruit in the commercial fruit orchards of the area. The author, Lynn, donned a coat and tie, a requirement in the Pomona public schools, and became a city kid.

The change in location and climate did not appear to improve the health of either Don or Pa, and within two years Pa decided to leave the area. In the spring of 1912, he sold the house on Hamilton Street and moved the family into temporary quarters a few blocks away while he searched for a new location. He had heard that the weather in the mountains north of Pomona was beneficial to asthmatics, and decided to relocate there. Early in April he loaded the family and their baggage into a dray and drove to the railway station of a small railroad serving the California mountain area. The ticket agent, however, told him the railroad would not allow Don, who was in a wheelchair and could not easily be maneuvered into a train coach, to ride in the baggage car as he had done on previous train trips. Pa felt those were unreasonable regulations, so instead of heading for the mountains he bought tickets to Nebraska on the line serving Nebraska via Denver (probably the Atcheson, Topeka, and Santa Fe). That line had no objection to Don's riding in the baggage car if he was attended by his younger brother, Lynn.

Ralph decided to return to Nebraska with the family and bought a ticket on the same train, but Glen had not saved enough money to afford passage, so Pa told him he would have to stay in Pomona and work until he could pay his own way.

A few days later the family arrived back at their old home in Nebraska. There they resumed farming the home farm, and Pa intermittently sold patent medicines, spices, tea, coffee, and cocoa, traveling from farmhouse to farmhouse with a team and closed wagon. Lynn took over operation of the farm a few years later and at this writing still lives on that same farm, where he was born.

Ralph held a number of farm jobs in Howard County until he died in 1923. Glen returned to Nebraska several months after the rest of the family arrived but did not move back into the family home, choosing instead to farm in northeastern Nebraska. He died in 1965 in Auburn, Washington. Bessie (Beck), the author's older sister, at this writing lives in Camas, Washington. Don's rheumatism continued to plague him, and he died at age twenty-eight in 1921.

Pa continued to suffer from asthma and periodically took solo trips to the West searching for relief. He spent at least one winter near Phoenix, Arizona, and several summers in the mountains of Colorado. In the fall of 1922, he and Ma caught a train to Colorado and spent the winter on the western slope of the Rockies, near Cedaredge. The next spring, believing life in the open air might benefit his health, he bought a covered wagon and a team of mules and he and Ma started up the trail to Steamboat Springs, Colorado, where he had earlier spent several summers. Early in May, 1923, his son-in-law in St. Paul received the following postal card:

Craig, Colo.

May 5th, 1923

Still on the pike. All well, and the roads are pretty good. 48 miles to Steamboat. Trying to rain today, and the weather is warm. Grass enough to feed the jacks. Write to Steamboat.—Dad

An undated newspaper clipping from an unidentified Steamboat Springs newspaper tells the rest of the story:

STRICKEN BY APOPLEXY ON ROAD FAR FROM HOME

W. H. Scott, aged 68, who owned valuable farm interests in the vicinity of St. Paul, Nebraska, died Saturday morning at the Steamboat hospital, less than 24 hours after he had suffered a cerebral hemorrhage while driving a team on the road between Hayden and Steamboat Springs. Mr. Scott, who was accompanied by his wife, spent last winter at Cedaredge, Delta County, and when warm weather approached they decided to come to Steamboat Springs for the summer, he being a great admirer of this locality, having spent several summers here during the past 12 years. The last time he was here was in 1920, and he is pleasantly remembered by many local residents. While here he made headquarters at the Shore cabins at the mouth of Soda Creek, but he spent considerable time at W. J. Mc-Causland's ranch on Hot Springs Creek. Mr. Scott had but one arm, having lost the other through an accident with a gun while he was a young man.

When Mrs. Scott realized that her husband had become seriously ill, she drove the team to the Wither ranch on Fourmile hill, and Earl Smith, manager of the property, brought them to Steamboat in his car. A son, W. R. Scott [W. W. Scott, ed.], arrived Sunday night from Hyannis, Nebr., and on Tuesday morning he and Mrs. Scott left for the eastern home, taking the remains of the dead father.

Friends agreed that he probably died as he would have wanted, on the trail behind a good team. After Pa's death, Ma lived with one or the other of her children in the St. Paul area until her death at sixty-nine in 1927.

Only five children figure prominently in *The Covered Wagon and Other Adventures*, but the author from time to time mentions older brothers and sisters. Four children—Della, Walter, Emma, and Josephine—all of whom were adults in 1906, did not accompany the family on their travels to Wyoming, Oregon, and California. Della (Dellie), born 1877, died at Broken Bow, Nebraska, in 1967. Walter (Walt, or Scotty), born 1881, who worked as a cowboy in western Nebraska when the family traveled to Wyoming, later became a ranch manager for Abbot Cattle Company. He died at St. Paul, Nebraska, in 1967. Emma (Em), born 1883, died at St. Paul in 1974. Josephine (Jose), born 1886, whose middle name was Samuel because Pa had wanted a boy, died at St. Paul in 1948.

Em and Jose had accompanied the family on an earlier, aborted covered wagon trip to California in 1900. In the spring of that year the family, accompanied by Pa's brother Jim and his wife and children, had started together to California, each family with its own "outfit." Pa would never force his teams to trot, preferring instead to let the horses set their own pace, so Jim, who was never known for his patience, became irritated with the slow pace and went on ahead. Ma had not been enthusiastic about the trip, for she was suffering the discomforts of what she thought was the onset of menopause. Somewhere in Wyoming or Colorado (their route across the Rockies is not known), Ma made the surprise announcement, "My 'change of life' just kicked me!" They promptly abandoned the trip and returned to Nebraska. Lynn was born five months later.

Lynn's children have long urged him to write an account of the two years the family spent in California, but he has resisted their pleas. "We were living as a city family there," he explains, "so we did not do everything together as we had done before. Ralph and Glen both were working, and I spent a lot of time with neighborhood kids. Any account I might write about those two years would be more about me than about the family. Besides," he adds, "my grandchildren will read it, and during that time I did a lot of things I would not want them to use as examples of how a boy should act."

Bill Scott